You can kill an **IDEA** . . .

but you can't kill an

OPPORTUNITY!

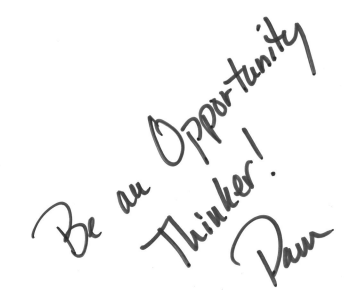

Be an Opportunity Thinker!

Pam

You can kill an **IDEA** . . . but you can't kill an **OPPORTUNITY!**

How to Discover **New Sources of Growth** for Your Organization

Pam Henderson, PhD

WILEY

Book layout and illustrations: Richard Merritt
Cover design: Nick Lippold

This book is printed on acid-free paper. ∞

Published by John Wiley & Sons, Inc., Hoboken, New Jersey.
Published simultaneously in Canada.

This text contains protected terminology, including Six Sources™, Opportunity Cartography™, Opportunity Landscape™, Opportunity Landscaping™, Opportunity Territories™, Opportunity Spaces™, Opportunity Thinking™, Opportunity Finders™, Six Sources of Opportunity™, Six Sources of Big Ideas™, Six Sources of Growth™, Rapid Brewery™, Killing Ideas™, You can kill and idea, you can't kill an opportunity!®, Opportunity Storming®, and Disruptive Market Research®.

For general information about our other products and services, please contact our Customer Care Department within the United States at (800) 762-2974, outside the United States at (317) 572-3993 or fax (317) 572-4002.

Wiley publishes in a variety of print and electronic formats and by print-on-demand. Some material included with standard print versions of this book may not be included in e-books or in print-on-demand. If this book refers to media such as a CD or DVD that is not included in the version you purchased, you may download this material at http://booksupport.wiley.com. For more information about Wiley products, visit www.wiley.com.

ISBN 978-1-118-80838-2 (pbk); ISBN 978-1-118-82274-6 (ebk); ISBN 978-1-118-82284-5 (ebk)

Printed in the United States of America

10 9 8 7 6 5 4 3 2 1

To:

The Author of everything

and

My amazingly creative, inspiring, and supportive family—
Michael, Bryce, Bond, Britt, and Mom.

You are
embarking
on a journey. . .

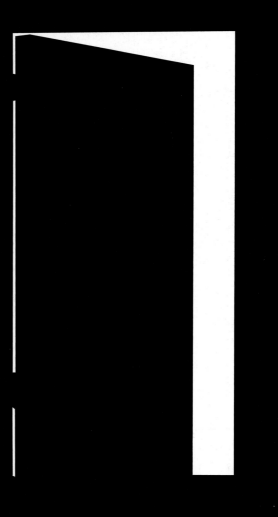

taking you around the world. . .

inspiring you with stories of organizations and brands...

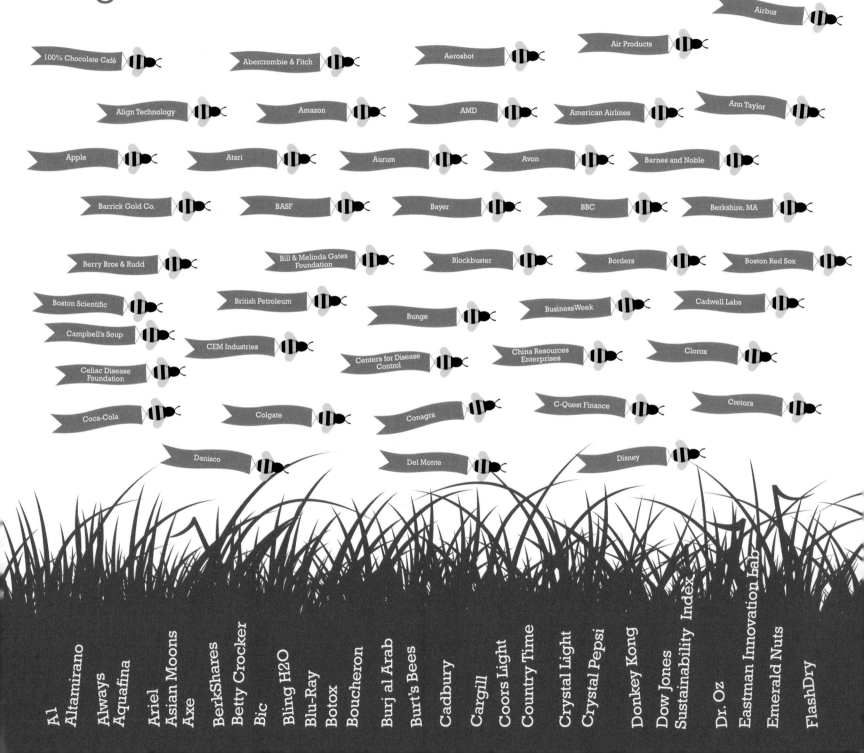

Airbus

100% Chocolate Café

Abercrombie & Fitch

Aeroshot

Air Products

Align Technology

Amazon

AMD

American Airlines

Ann Taylor

Apple

Atari

Aurum

Avon

Barnes and Noble

Barrick Gold Co.

BASF

Bayer

BBC

Berkshire, MA

Berry Bros & Rudd

Bill & Melinda Gates Foundation

Blockbuster

Borders

Boston Red Sox

Boston Scientific

British Petroleum

Bunge

BusinessWeek

Cadwell Labs

Campbell's Soup

CEM Industries

China Resources Enterprises

Clorox

Celiac Disease Foundation

Centers for Disease Control

Coca-Cola

Colgate

Conagra

C-Quest Finance

Cretors

Danisco

Del Monte

Disney

A1
Altamirano
Always
Aquafina
Ariel
Asian Moons
Axe
BerkShares
Betty Crocker
Bic
Bling H2O
Blu-Ray
Botox
Boucheron
Burj al Arab
Burt's Bees
Cadbury
Cargill
Coors Light
Country Time
Crystal Light
Crystal Pepsi
Donkey Kong
Dow Jones Sustainability Index
Dr. Oz
Eastman Innovation Lab
Emerald Nuts
FlashDry

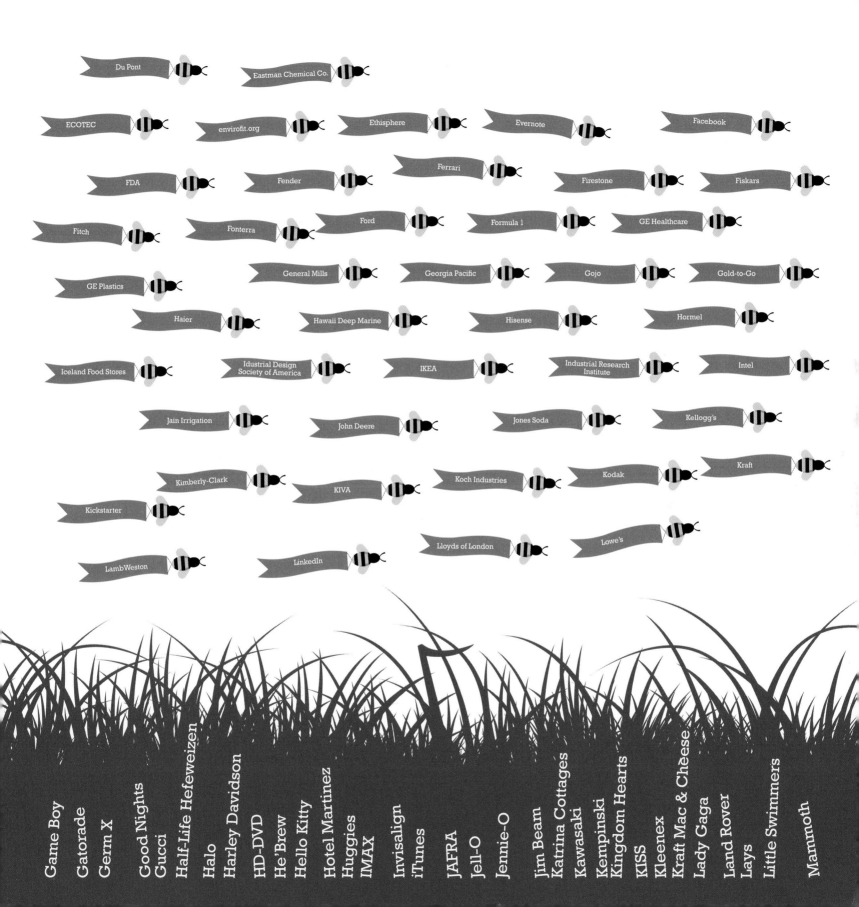

Du Pont

Eastman Chemical Co.

ECOTEC

envirofit.org

Ethisphere

Evernote

Facebook

FDA

Fender

Ferrari

Firestone

Fiskars

Fitch

Fonterra

Ford

Formula 1

GE Healthcare

GE Plastics

General Mills

Georgia Pacific

Gojo

Gold-to-Go

Haier

Hawaii Deep Marine

Hisense

Hormel

Iceland Food Stores

Idustrial Design
Society of America

IKEA

Industrial Research
Institute

Intel

Jain Irrigation

John Deere

Jones Soda

Kellogg's

Kimberly-Clark

KIVA

Koch Industries

Kodak

Kraft

Kickstarter

Lloyds of London

Lowe's

LambWeston

LinkedIn

Game Boy
Gatorade
Germ X
Good Nights
Gucci
Half-Life Hefeweizen
Halo
Harley Davidson
HD-DVD
He'Brew
Hello Kitty
Hotel Martinez
Huggies
IMAX
Invisalign
iTunes
JAFRA
Jell-O
Jennie-O
Jim Beam
Katrina Cottages
Kawasaki
Kempinski
Kingdom Hearts
KISS
Kleenex
Kraft Mac & Cheese
Lady Gaga
Land Rover
Lays
Little Swimmers
Mammoth

in pursuit of opportunity and growth. . .

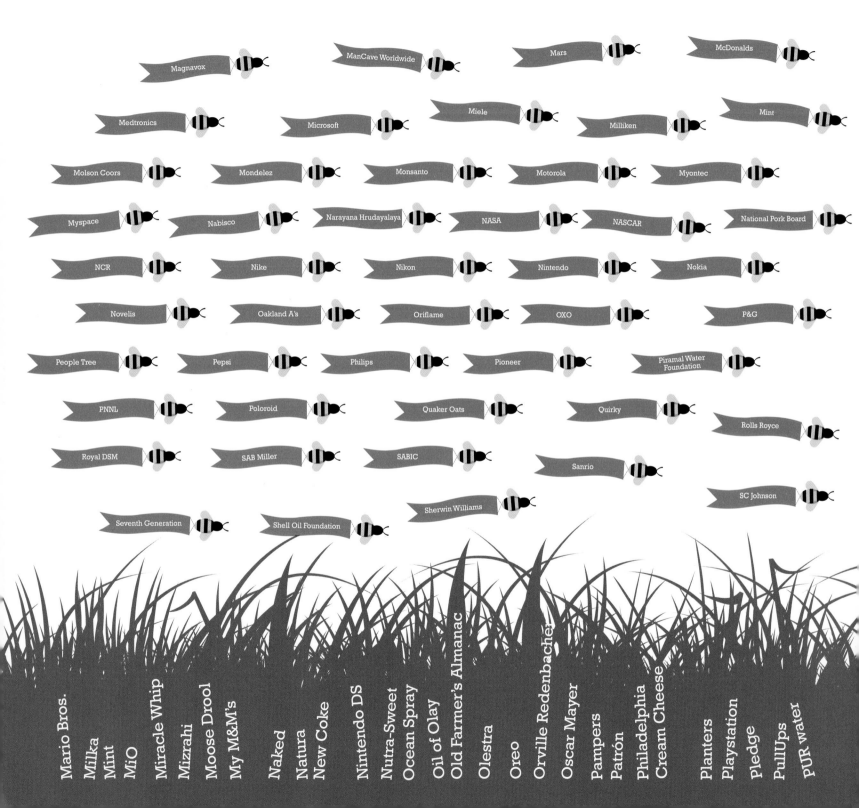

Magnavox
ManCave Worldwide
Mars
McDonalds
Medtronics
Microsoft
Miele
Milliken
Mint
Molson Coors
Mondelez
Monsanto
Motorola
Myontec
Myspace
Nabisco
Narayana Hrudayalaya
NASA
NASCAR
National Pork Board
NCR
Nike
Nikon
Nintendo
Nokia
Novelis
Oakland A's
Oriflame
OXO
P&G
People Tree
Pepsi
Philips
Pioneer
Piramal Water Foundation
PNNL
Poloroid
Quaker Oats
Quirky
Rolls Royce
Royal DSM
SAB Miller
SABIC
Sanrio
SC Johnson
Seventh Generation
Shell Oil Foundation
Sherwin Williams

Mario Bros.
Milka
Mint
MiO
Miracle Whip
Mizrahi
Moose Drool
My M&M's
Naked
Natura
New Coke
Nintendo DS
Nutra-Sweet
Ocean Spray
Oil of Olay
Old Farmer's Almanac
Olestra
Oreo
Orville Redenbacher
Oscar Mayer
Pampers
Patrón
Philadelphia Cream Cheese
Planters
Playstation
Pledge
PullUps
PUR water

toward a bigger future through Opportunity Thinking!

CHAPTER 1

BIG THINKING

This book is about growth . . .

growth that starts by killing ideas.

Killing ideas that **won't lead to growth**.
Killing ideas as **the starting point for growth**.

Killing ideas in order to **begin at**
the real starting place for growth—

opportunity.

Opportunity which, when truly understood,
provides **clues** to building the right ideas—

big ideas.

Big ideas, killer ideas that produce

big growth.

A paradox?

Not really.

Ideas have too often been relied upon as the catalyst for growth.

Why not? Ideas are enticing, ideas are entertaining, and ideas are energizing. Each good one holds hope—hope for a better world, for a fuller life, for things bigger, faster, cheaper, healthier, more beautiful—hope for some kind of tangible growth.

We hunger for ideas to help meet our challenges, solve our problems, and give us a brighter future. Without ideas there would be little progress. History is full of amazing ideas that have delivered both small and large advances in how we live. Many of these successes were so noteworthy and so beneficial we eventually began to assume ideas were the source of progress and the creators of growth.

"

Ideas are any
man's greatest asset.

Harvey Firestone, founder of Firestone Tires

Ideas are the beginning points
of all fortunes.

Napoleon Hill, personal success guru

It's always possible to
have a great company if
you have great ideas.

Jerry Yang, co-founder of Yahoo!

Ideas . . . more than money, are
the real currency for success.

Eli Broad, billionaire, philanthropist

Real wealth is
ideas plus energy.

Richard Buckminster Fuller, architect, futurist

"

Despite their allure, ideas in the commercial world are too often failing to deliver on their promises.

It takes about 3,000 ideas to get 100 projects, which result in only two launches, producing, on average, one product that breaks even. Of these products, only 20% make some appreciable profit!

Considering all the commercial ideas we generate, the vast majority aren't very good after all. Ideas are more likely to disappoint than delight, becoming an expensive distraction from growth. This is not the result of acting hastily. The average length of a major new product development project in most industries is measured in years, not months.

We are dismally failing with our ideas, even after we have plenty of time to examine them. This is not only a waste of time, resources, and investment but also a waste of personal commitment.

3,000
ideas leading to

100
projects resulting in

2
launches, of which

1
breaks even

It's been said that no idea is a bad idea. This brainstorming mantra is meant to spur creativity and unleash a torrent of ideas by removing barriers of doubt and objection. We all know it isn't true, though—some ideas are actually quite bad!

The problem is not with the mantra; the problem is that we don't have a reliable way of producing or knowing a good idea from a bad one until it's too late. As a result, in a world dying to have new ideas, new ideas are all too often dying and taking our hopes and aspirations for growth down with them.

If bad ideas were to have an epitaph it would probably be . . .

R.I.P.

WELL, IT SEEMED
LIKE A GOOD IDEA
AT THE TIME.

Clearly our concern here is not with ideas that fail in the lab. After all, Thomas Edison—a master of invention—is credited with saying of his pursuit of the lightbulb,

"I haven't failed; I've just found 10,000 ways that won't work."

It is important to form many ideas and to test them—in the lab. Our concern is with those that fail in the market—the ideas on which we place our bets for success and profit and send forth with great anticipation into the world. These ideas passed the lab tests but failed the wallet test, disappointing us and our customers.

So what distinguishes ideas that succeed in delivering growth from those that don't?

Some ideas fail because there appears to be no demand for them.

People weren't clamoring for Tangy Fish and Crispy Bacon flavored water for their pets; parents were offended by Abercrombie and Fitch's introduction of padded swimsuit tops for little girls; and no one seemed to find disposable underwear from Bic to be compelling enough to buy. There have been a stream of tech flops, from Microsoft's ActiMates, plush toys that connected children to TV programmers (a bit scary!); to Sony's egg-shaped Rolly, their contender for the iPod; or Swatch's Internet Time, a new system for telling time with 1,000 beats, meant to reduce the confusion of time zones. Never heard of these? Well, that's the point!

The list of ideas that didn't last in the market could fill these pages. From New Coke to Crystal Pepsi, otherwise successful companies and people have too often missed the mark, either in concept or timing.

Other ideas intrigued us with hints at success: they had all of us watching, even expecting them to revolutionize the world, but ultimately they went out with a whimper. They failed because they caught the edge of an opportunity, but a better-crafted alternative captured the full potential.

Experts and amateurs alike closely followed the Blu-ray versus HD-DVD battle. Although Toshiba's HD-DVD could be produced at lower cost, a Blu-ray disc played on more popular devices, such as the Sony PlayStation console, and carried a wider movie library. Car-sharing programs, such as Zipcar, delivered a solution for inner-city transport by using the existing infrastructure around cars while foot-traffic replacements like the Segway drowned in strict regulations, limited uses, and high costs. Highly promoted and highly processed fat alternative, Olestra, was quickly shunned by consumers ultimately favoring the simple, natural solution of baked snacks from Lays.

These ideas didn't take root: like tumbleweeds, they died and were blown away. Some were planted where there was no opportunity and others were not sufficiently rooted where there was opportunity. Ideas that fully tap into opportunity are far more likely to take hold and fulfill their promise of growth. **It is the opportunity that both predefines the value of an idea and defines those ideas that will have value.**

We need to start with opportunity.

Of course, it makes sense that relying on ideas rather than opportunities is like putting the cart before the horse.

But if this is so well understood, why do we, by all appearances, hitch our hopes to ideas rather than opportunities?

After all, many innovation processes start with ideation. Business leaders spend hours in idea-generation sessions but little time in opportunity-generation sessions. Myriad methodologies have been published on ideation, but few exist on opportunity definition.

Is it any wonder that the most common image on the cover of any innovation book is the lightbulb, the icon for the "bright idea"?

Some organizations have clearly invested in exploring opportunity, but most only give a head nod to its definition. From innovation to acquisition, business processes require some sort of description of the potential opportunity prize and an approximation of its size. Unfortunately, the ensuing opportunity stories are usually thin at best, lacking any real depth, and provide little direction for developing, let alone choosing, the ideas that will succeed.

We tick the opportunity box by requiring estimates of opportunity size, using metrics such as total available market, potential market share, or some other measure.

The size merely tells us go or no-go. It leaves us in the dark about true opportunity (who, what, where, when, and why), giving us little direction as to its real attractiveness or fit and even less direction toward which ideas will work.

Without this information, even the numbers are suspect. How can we really seize an opportunity when we know so little about it? This may be one reason why as many as 80% of mergers and acquisitions don't live up to expectations. Leaders envision a transformed company created from an acquisition, but the changing of the guard may not even phase the market, delivering no new value to customers and, in the end, no new value to shareholders. Lack of clarity on the dynamics of an opportunity contributes to missing the mark in other areas of business as well. We risk wasting marketing dollars, developing new brands that fall flat, creating brand extensions that cannibalize revenue, and pursuing geographic expansions that are later retracted. We may have figured out the size of the opportunity, carefully calculating financial returns, but have no notion of its real nature.

Knowing how much water a vase will hold doesn't tell us anything about its shape, much less what flowers it's best suited to display.

Knowing the size of an opportunity doesn't tell us anything about its shape much less the ideas that will best fit.

We must go beyond sizing as a proxy for understanding opportunity and dig deeper into its real nature. Currently, opportunity exploration and idea generation are separate processes, completely disconnected from each other. Understanding opportunities should be the foundation for developing ideas that resonate in the market.

The problems with ideas and their lack of success are driving people to say they want bigger ideas. But bigger ideas simply don't happen without bigger opportunities and a better understanding of those opportunities.

Think of an idea as a koi and an opportunity as the pond. Some suggest if you put one of these beautiful orange and black Japanese fish in a small pond, it will stay small. Put it in a large pond and that same fish will grow quite large. The fish grow only as large as their environment allows.

If we want a big fish, we need a big pond; and if we want a big idea, we need a big opportunity.

While many organizations have realized the importance of killing off individual ideas in order to arrive at bigger ideas, they have not come to understand that ideas themselves might be the culprit for their lower-than-expected returns. The allure of ideas has distracted us from understanding opportunity. Too often, ideas have been disguised as the path to growth when in fact they have been a path to nowhere. Something has to change. We must stop hoping for the BIG IDEA that will kick-start our growth. Instead we need to start our growth journey focused on discovering and generating opportunity as the precursor to big ideas.

This book isn't big-growth nirvana. It won't give all the answers or point to fields lush with opportunities. It won't guarantee winning, but it can improve your odds and reduce your risk. What this book will do is unfold the unique approach of Opportunity Thinking, which could dramatically change the way you pursue growth and develop really big ideas.

Killing ideas *as* the starting point for growth *is* the starting point for growth.

Opportunity is the path to killer ideas.

You can kill an idea, but you can't kill an opportunity!

CHAPTER 2

BIG
GROWTH

One of the pleasures in a child's life is to track their progress of growth on a wall with pencil markings. Our desire for growth begins early and doesn't stop with childhood. Growth evokes a spirit of optimism for a promising future. Whether we are running a business, getting an education, raising children, or tending a garden, growth is a key measure of success.

Today's organizations also want growth, particularly at a time when it seems so hard to come by. Growth is a signal of a healthy business. It draws in stockholders, gives confidence to stakeholders, engages employees in new challenges and pursuits, and appeals to customers. Growth is a sign we are doing the right things for today and the future.

march 13

08.12

04.23.12

09 2011

03.10

05 09

26th
Nov 08

07 08

66If it's not growing, it's going to die.99

Michael Eisner, former CEO of Disney

Growth is in the eye of the beholder

Organizations seek to grow in different ways at different times. Companies might target market share or revenues, focus on profitability or geographic footprint.

But growth doesn't always mean size.

In a world that is questioning the limits of growth, growth can mean an organization has broader impact on people while using fewer resources, creates bigger innovations from fewer projects, builds a stronger reputation and a larger community, or does more good with its current assets.

Most organizations want something more. They don't want just growth by the numbers; they want growth beyond the numbers—transformational growth that strengthens and builds their organization, culture, and impact.

This is big growth—growth that touches the organization more deeply and provides a springboard for the future, ensuring that the growth will be sustainable.

Sustainable growth is hard to come by, even for seasoned and successful companies. Organizations that appear to be at the top of their game and to have cornered the market on their opportunities do not always stay at the top.

When the Fortune 500 list began in 1955, historical data predicted that companies would average 75 years on the list. By 1983 the lifespan on the list had fallen to 40 years. Today it is 15 years; and 434 of the original 500 have fallen off the list—all in a little more than 50 years.

Several of today's most respected and innovative companies didn't exist 15 years ago. Chances are they, too, will be replaced, probably sooner than their founders think.

So what happened to those who are gone? Their growth was not sustainable. Perhaps they tapped out their opportunities; and as the opportunities dried up so did their drive. Maybe risk aversion grew with prominence; complacency grew with success; or the politics of the parts overshadowed the imperative of the whole. Some may have assumed that big growth was perpetual—a right—based on the growth they had already achieved. In the end, many failed to change while others innovated and developed even more imaginative ways to capture the hearts and minds of customers.

75

40

15

"The most fatal illusion is the narrow point of view. Since life is growth and motion, a fixed point of view kills anybody who has one."

Brooks Atkinson, theater critic

Sustainable growth comes from many forces, but it starts with identifying sustainable opportunities. Such opportunities have both depth and longevity. They are big enough to ensure they won't be tapped out in the near future. They allow for more than a one-hit wonder, creating room for a true pipeline of big ideas.

Sustainable growth also comes from recognizing that opportunities don't stand still. Opportunities are constantly morphing and taking on new forms. To grow sustainably, we must be followers of opportunities and change as they change.

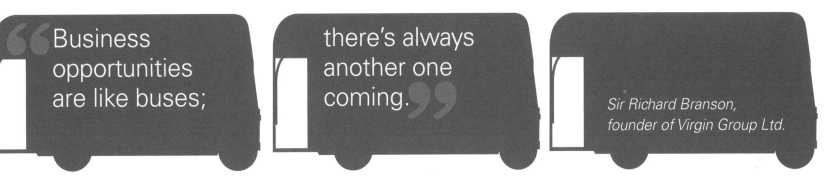

"Business opportunities are like buses; there's always another one coming."

Sir Richard Branson, founder of Virgin Group Ltd.

Ability to follow opportunity and adapt accordingly is driven, in part, by the vision of leaders and the culture they help create. Encouraging an organization to follow opportunity as it changes requires courage and a willingness to constantly transform—an uneasy act when organizations themselves are also shifting and changing faster than ever before.

130 directorships, including CEO, CFO, and so on, will change in the next 60 minutes

In many organizations roles change on an annual basis, making the process of guiding the organization through changing opportunities even more difficult. It can even become attractive from a career standpoint to risk future growth in order to look good today, consigning sustainable growth to whoever may follow.

Sustaining growth requires a balancing act of following opportunity and not getting ahead of it.

If we try to grow too fast, we will not be able to sustain growth. Growing too fast is just as dangerous as being sluggish in following our opportunities. We see this in agriculture. If we underfertilize, plants won't reach their full potential in yield. If we overfertilize, plants will become stalky, leggy, unable to support the fruit they produce. Either way, an organization won't be making the most of opportunity and won't sustain proper growth.

Growth can not only outstrip our opportunities and organizations, but also our environment. Big, sustainable growth provides for today in a way that does not exhaust what will be needed tomorrow. It means allowing our resources to regenerate or evolve so that we may draw from them in the future. It takes responsibility for the ethical, social, and economic impact upon our employees and the wider community. Companies can certainly grow without acting responsibly, but usually it will come back to harm them. Alternatively, no company can afford to grow in a way that is great for the environment but so expensive or inefficient that it cannot sustain its business. That is why many companies are now looking at the triple bottom line—profits, people, and planet. Our goal must be to identify opportunities that will reward responsible growth and create ways to grow responsibly wherever we are.

Seventh Generation has found and expanded opportunity for sustainable growth across the triple bottom line. They sell consumer goods including cleaning, baby care, and personal care products. Their mission is to inspire a revolution that nurtures the health of the next seven generations. Reduced waste and less toxicity in formulation and packaging has been their product development focus, earning them the U.S. Food and Drug Administration's Bio-Approval label.

An extensive range of corporate responsibility programs—from their efforts to reduce greenhouse gases to their partnerships with Latina women's organizations to raise women out of poverty—won them the prestigious Leader for Change award from the United Nations in 2011. They even teach courses on their "for-benefit model," a business model in which for-profit companies create social and environmental benefits. The reward for Seventh Generation has been sales that have grown 160% since beginning business in 1988.

> "In our every deliberation, we must consider the impact of our decisions on the next seven generations."
>
> *Great Law of the Iroquois Confederacy*

Sustainable, responsible growth can come from different strategies. Some companies pursue this growth through evolutionary approaches while others seek to grow through revolutionary efforts.

Evolutionary approach to opportunity

Evolutionary strategies for growth come from tapping into the depths of an opportunity through our current approaches to creating value. We stick with an opportunity and mine it, creating growth from it, and continually building from our core.

We pursue ways to improve our products, reduce costs, enhance technology, or stretch brands. An evolutionary approach to opportunity is no less rewarding than its more radical-sounding counterpart: revolution. Evolutionary strategies can produce as significant growth over time as revolutionary strategies—much like the tortoise beating the hare.

Evolutionary approaches to growth are not without their challenges, though. We might imagine that because growth is close to home we would know our opportunities well enough to know a good idea when we see it. Not so. Opportunities we sit within are often the most difficult to understand.

Just as a fish doesn't know it is wet, so companies often can't see or feel the very opportunities where they are swimming.

Perhaps this is why line extensions underdeliver against current products by over 13% in revenue, cannibalizing current product sales and reducing total revenue. Companies find it difficult to move beyond their core products, varieties, or flavors. Nothing beats the original.

Understanding how to dig deeper in our current opportunities requires fresh eyes and fresh approaches to produce big ideas that help us better mine potential.

🌱 Fiskars illustrates how to continually apply core capabilities to grow opportunity. Fiskars Ironworks is Finland's oldest company and one of the oldest in the world. Started in 1649 in the Uusimaa province of Finland, they literally mined opportunity—beginning with iron and later with the discovery of copper. They focused on producing metal items, starting with nails and wires, then steam engines and tools.

Their excellence in metal tools brought new growth. In the 1960s, Olaf Backstrom, a Fiskars engineer, experimented with strip stainless steel and injection-molded plastics, and designed the world's first lightweight scissors, complete with their now-signature orange plastic handles. Aesthetically pleasing, the design won them a position in the Design Collection of the Museum of Modern Art in New York.

At one point they tried to grow through acquisitions further from their core, but backed off when these attempts eroded profits. Restructuring and focusing on acquisitions in tools and metal items led to success. They have steadily grown their market position and sales of everything from scissors to garden equipment. Their approach to sustainability has emerged directly from their core—driven through enduring design and attention to materials, as well as the low carbon footprint and end-of-life of their products. 🌱

Evolutionary approaches to growing within our opportunities allow us to do what we do well and expand carefully into adjacent applications. These approaches can bring big rewards for companies in terms of efficiency and know-how.

🌱 Consider WD-40's approach to mining its opportunities. In 1953 the company developed a water-resistant chemical intended for sale to a niche market of large industrial rocket producers. The product found its way into a few employees' homes where it was used to oil hinges and more. WD-40 repackaged the substance for retail distribution in 1958. The lubricant's market share grew steadily with the introduction of new applications. Starting with three employees, the company has become a lean machine of a mere 280 employees managing over $300 million in sales annually, with presence in 80% of U.S. households. A determined focus has paid off handsomely with consistent growth. 🌱

Revolutionary approach to opportunity

Revolutionary approaches to growth come from either creating a new opportunity or from radically expanding an opportunity by changing how we deliver value. This type of approach could come from breakthrough innovation in technology, opening new markets, utilizing resources that were sitting idle, delivering a new business model, or acquiring a new capability. Revolution occurs when we create a breakthrough or when we take advantage of an adjacent breakthrough. Technologies such as the Internet, smartphones and social media have transformed how almost every business pursues opportunity.

Revolutionary strategies smack of big ideas—killer ideas so big that they, in and of themselves, expand opportunity. These ideas usually create new value for consumers, expanding the original opportunity while also attracting a following of new competitors. Sometimes in an effort to pursue revolutionary growth we venture into opportunities that feel so foreign they all look big and exciting. Not all of them are attractive, but we lack the frame of reference to know a good one from a bad one. Ignorance can make everything look innovative! Just because a business model or product offering is new to us doesn't mean it will bring truly new value to a market, even if it threatens to create disruption among our own staff. Successful growth from revolution requires that we revolutionize our markets or industries, as opposed to inciting revolution within our own companies.

Some of the most successful revolution happens when we upend the current ways of doing things in established industries, combining several forms of innovation to capture opportunity in a new way.

Revolutionizing an old industry is the story of **IKEA**.

🌳 Started in 1943 by 17-year-old Ingvar Kampred in Sweden, IKEA (named after his initials and that of the farm he grew up on) soon began selling inexpensive, locally made, quality wood furniture. When he outgrew his shop, he started a catalog with mail order and deliveries made by milkmen! To defend against competitors, he created a showroom to demonstrate the quality of his surprisingly economical furniture. In 1956, seeing the struggles of customers to transport what they bought, IKEA redesigned furniture to allow easy carrying, disassembly, and flat packing. Expansion was gradual at first—Norway, Denmark, and Switzerland. With a focus on reducing costs, they innovated on their supply chain, buying sawmills, developing rail systems, and integrating from forest to furniture. Design, functionality, and materials were continually improved to create superior aesthetics and usability. Their mix of new approaches led to explosive growth, with stores opening across Western and Eastern Europe, Australia, the United States, Japan, China, and more. They grew so fast they accidentally opened a store in the wrong city. With more than 280 stores in more than 25 countries, sales have reached €25 billion (about $33.4 billion) with €2.9 billion (about $3.9 billion) in net income, making IKEA the world's largest furniture retailer and the third-largest consumer of wood in the world, behind Lowe's and The Home Depot!

The model that won them growth is delivering a great sustainability record. In 2010 they redesigned a popular sofa, the EKTOR, reducing pack size by 50%, eliminating 7,400 trucks and reducing CO_2 emissions by 4,700 tons per year. Partnering with the World Wildlife Foundation, across their integrated value chain they are taking on issues such as cotton cultivation, water treatment, and forestry management. With a goal of running on 100% renewable energy, they are building a wind farm and have investments in alternative energy ranging from solar to geothermal. They and their customers have donated more than €82 million (about $107 million) to children's education, prevention of child labor, and relief in more than 20 countries. 🌳

Revolutionary growth can start in unexpected places—sometimes leveraging abundant resources that have heretofore gone unused—creating new opportunity.

🌳 Saudi Arabia had an abundance of natural gas from oil production, gas which was just being flared or reinjected. Equally abundant was their labor force, eager for growth. The government saw an opportunity to add value to both. In 1976 they established the Saudi Basic Industries Corporation (SABIC) to produce chemicals, polymers, and fertilizers. SABIC soon became one of the world's fastest growing and most profitable companies, going from production of 6.3 million metric tons (mmt) in 1985 to 69 mmt by 2012. Sales are now SR190B (about $50 billion) with net income of SR29B (about $7.7 billion). They have created jobs and educational assistance both at home and in 40 other countries where they are located.

Innovation in plastics has won them top awards in sustainability for their high performance iQ resin, a proprietary product produced from recycled polyethylene terephthalate (PET) bottles. The material requires half the CO_2 to produce and, combined with SABIC's color-matching abilities, can be used in applications ranging from furniture to computers to automobiles. Innovating with Land Rover, they combined their polymers with efficient design to cut the Evoque's weight by 35%, reducing fuel consumption and CO_2 emissions, while improving the wear, strength, and aesthetics of the parts. 🌳

Revolution meets evolution

Some opportunities lend themselves to evolution from continuous improvement, while others are ripe for revolution from breakthrough. However, opportunities do not stand still. They are often on the move. They may look dormant for a time and then burst forth, opening the doors for new growth but also new competition.

The changing face of opportunity challenges a conundrum we see in growth literature and boardrooms. Should we grow close to the core through continuous improvement in capabilities and markets or further from the core by expanding and seeking breakthrough in our technologies or markets? This decision can make or break a company. In fact, a new CEO will sometimes swing the pendulum from one side of the debate to the other, shifting resources closer to or further from the company's center of gravity.

This is a bit of a false dilemma. When we look at growth through the eyes of opportunity we realize that we can only grow in accordance with the nature of the opportunity itself, and the nature of all opportunities is that they change. They have a life of their own regardless of our predispositions. Once revolutionized into existence, an opportunity will be developed through evolution until conditions are ripe for revolution once more. This means we must be agile enough to grow both close to our core and beyond if we are to sustain growth from opportunity. The shifts required by this cycle can catch us off guard. We often struggle to see the potential for revolution when we are working hard on evolutionary growth. We rarely ask, "How can we obsolete ourselves?" Although we should ask ourselves this question if we hope to sustain our growth.

If we neglect to keep an eye on the shifting sands of the opportunity landscape, we will be left aiming at a mirage while our opportunity has dried up or moved on, leaving our growth aspirations in the dust.

Long dormant, China recently became one of the fastest growing beer markets in the world. The opportunity in China can be seen in two companies—one with evolutionary growth, the other with revolutionary growth.

🍂 Tsingtao is a picture of the last 100 years of China itself. Established in 1903 by the Germans who had invaded China, it was acquired by the Japanese in 1914 and turned back into a Chinese-owned brewery in 1922. In 1949 it was taken over by the People's Republic of China and privatized later, in the 1990s. Largely exported until the 1980s, it is the number one Chinese beer in many international markets. It has been a mature beer waiting for the domestic market to catch up.

As happens with opportunities, they change; and with that change new competition arises. The newcomer Xue Hua, known as Snow, was formed in 1993 through a joint venture between China Resources Enterprises and SAB Miller. Snow has grown through acquisition and by leapfrogging with technology—taking old breweries and upgrading them with the best technology. They have focused on brand building—targeting youth and linking their brand to growing activities, such as skiing, a sport where the number of resorts alone has doubled in just a few years.

Revolutionary approaches to an opportunity can sometimes overtake evolutionary approaches, displacing those who built the market to start with. Snow is now the larger of the two beer companies. It hasn't just leapfrogged Tsingtao, though. It has leapfrogged all other beers in the world—becoming the best-selling beer of all! 🍂

Opportunity is the engine for growth.

Opportunities are often on the move.

Growth both close to and far from our core will be necessary if we are to be followers of opportunity.

CHAPTER 3

BIG
OPPORTUNITY

Opportunity: origin 1375–1425 [Latin *ob portu*]

The word opportunity harkens back to a world of harbors and sailing vessels. Before the chug of an engine could power a boat to safe harbor, sailing ships had to sit outside of port waiting for the right wind and tide conditions to carry them and their wares to their destination. These conditions were called *ob portu*, Latin for "into port." The perfect mix of tide and wind conditions came to be called opportunity.

Ask around today and many would say that the opportunity was the port itself—the market awaiting the goods—the people with unmet needs, wants, and desires creating demand for new products from distant lands. At the other side of the world, the maker of the goods that became cargo may have viewed the opportunity as the chance to invent something new, perhaps using a new technology to create superior goods, which in turn spurred new demand. The people of that time saw it differently. To them the opportunity was about the conditions that brought the cargo and the port together.

Real opportunity lies in all three—the port awaiting the goods, the capabilities and technologies that make those goods possible, and the weather and tides that bring them together. In times past, as well as today, opportunity for revenue is only realized when all three coincide. One without the other is hardly an opportunity. Revenue is not possible when people in the port long for goods that can neither be created nor ever arrive. The technologies and abilities to create goods neither guarantee a receptive market nor ships that will safely sail. Bright sunny days with favorable winds and tides may be lovely to bask in but won't make anyone money without a boat full of cargo and an eager harbor awaiting new wares.

Opportunity for revenue combines a receptive audience, the capabilities to create the right value, and the conditions that bring them together. The combination of the three is what ultimately yields revenue.

Opportunity for revenue does not guarantee revenue, of course. There is still the need for ingenuity and hard work to create the right products and services, touch the right customers, and take advantage of the conditions in the environment. These activities result from a plethora of imaginative ideas and an enormous amount of skillful, hard work. Ideas translate an opportunity for revenue into money in the bank. Yet, if not spurred and surrounded by the best opportunity conditions, ideas themselves are powerless to deliver returns.

Consider the champion of ideas:

the lightbulb.

It is both a big idea
and our metaphor
for big ideas.

The lightbulb evokes an image of the electricity of our thoughts powering the bright ideas of our imagination. While it is a brilliant invention, it would be nothing if it weren't for an inherent desire for light and the dissatisfaction with candles and lanterns that created a market willing to pay for a better solution. Nor would it even be possible if it weren't for technologies that preceded it, from blowing glass to the development of the original carbon filaments that were heated until they glowed. It was not a singular invention. It took years from the invention of the original lightbulb in the early 1800s by Humphry Davy until Thomas Edison invented a longer lasting, marketable bulb in 1879. Finally, none of this would have come to pass without an environment where electricity was accessible and a significant gas lighting infrastructure had proved that widespread adoption of a similar technology could work.

The opportunity for the lightbulb was monumental and, as with many opportunities, it has continued to grow and morph, getting even bigger. The lightbulb itself is just a glass bulb of argon gas around a tungsten filament; the true opportunity is for more reliable and available illumination, a longer day, and an infinite cascade of human and cultural benefits.

Stories abound of such great and singular inventions as the lightbulb. The inventors and visionaries behind them have become our heroes of creativity. However, further scrutiny reveals that their ideas had the good fortune to meet up with opportunity. Some of us may call the inventors lucky, others insightful, gifted, persistent, or creative, but the ones who are remembered are those whose inventions coincided with opportunity. Thus when their ideas or improvements won, they won big. While the idea and its originator receive the credit, the real origin of revenue was the opportunity.

Opportunity often sits in the background, while the idea and its inventor take center stage. But the opportunity is what gives the idea a chance to achieve stardom.

It is understandable why ideas grab the limelight. They are easier to see than opportunities—easier to describe, visualize, and grasp. Developing ideas is completely within our control—developing opportunities is not. Perhaps this is why we often gravitate toward ideation before we fully understand the opportunity. Opportunity conditions are more complex and difficult to articulate. Still, as complex as opportunities may seem, they can be unraveled in systematic ways.

OPPORTUNITY

Exploring Opportunity

Exploring opportunity is far from a uniquely modern pursuit. People throughout history have expanded their opportunities through courageous and creative endeavors. Explorers of old searched for new ports. Businesses expanded what they could make and take to those markets. They searched for new technologies to create products so novel and useful that even stranded cargo would be taken into port by rowboat. They created ways to mark their goods with unique symbols so they could expand via a growing reputation. They innovated on how to finance their ventures by seeking both individual investors and the crown purse to expand to new lands. Ship makers and sailors learned ways to leverage the tide and winds through changes to their vessels and sails. These merchants and explorers knew **opportunity was not just found; it could also be created and expanded.**

We, too, can find and expand opportunity by exploring new markets, adopting new ways of making things, building our reputations through how we express our brands, attempting new ways of doing business, and leveraging the conditions around us that influence our ability to successfully bring together the value we create with the people we hope to serve. Opportunity comes from the combination of many efforts and forces. Both today and in the past we see several primary sources of potential that reflect the way we create value, the people hungering for that value, and the various conditions that govern how the two come together.

The **people** we serve are obviously our *markets* but also people within our *organizations* seeking better ways to create value and profit from it. The broader *environment* also has people we serve including the culture, regulators, and influencers.

The ways we create **value** span the *technologies* we develop, the way our *organizations* produce what we develop, how we choose to monetize the value through our *business model*, and how we *express* ourselves through our *design*, brand image, and positioning.

The **conditions** that govern how the two come together span both the way we create value and the people that will benefit—the competing and complementary *technologies, organizations, brands*, and *business models*; the nature of our *markets*; and cultural, regulatory, economic, and natural *environments*.

These define the six primary sources of opportunity.

OPPORTUNITY THINKING

Opportunity combines:

- a receptive audience,

- the capabilities to create value, and

- the conditions that bring them together.

All three are required to achieve revenue.

BIG
SOURCES

The Six Sources of Opportunity are our technologies, brand expression, business models, organizations, market, and environment.

About the time the term *ob portu* came into being (1375–1425) opportunity itself was exploding. The world was expanding. Western Europeans were looking for new routes to the East to satiate their appetites for spices and silk.

Demand for spices meant demand for better boats—boats that could sail faster and into the winds of the Atlantic—and this spurred massive growth in the shipbuilding industry. Ships with square sails were replaced with the caravel, born from observing the triangular sails of African fishing boats. The ship required new materials for sail cloth, ropes, and waterproofing. It also required fewer, more skilled sailors to operate—sailors who knew how to tack into the southern winds. Funding for shipbuilding increased with monies coming from governments and merchants. Ships sailed under the flags of Portugal and Spain each racing to build their reputations and wealth.

Equally critical for growth in exploration was a change in culture, attitudes, and beliefs. However, there was a bit of a problem. Many people feared that if they ventured out into the Atlantic they would meet up with sea monsters, whirlpools, boiling waters, and searing sun. This was a bit of a deterrent to most! But Gil Eanes changed everything. In 1434 he managed to round, and more importantly return unscathed from Cape Bojador on the coast of Africa, proving that the Atlantic was safer than thought. This singular event kick-started Portuguese exploration of Africa.

The new technologies combined with demand from merchants, new funding sources and new ways to staff ships, empire building, and changes in the culture were the stuff that opportunity was made of. The same stuff opportunity is made of today. Across this opportunity and opportunity in general, we see Six Sources of Opportunity.

Throughout history, organizations and individuals have developed fresh approaches to idea generation and opportunity exploration within each of the Six Sources. We've seen approaches from design thinking to business model generation and from lean manufacturing to blue ocean strategies.

Each of these perspectives can stretch and enrich insight into opportunity, revealing that opportunity does indeed spring from many Sources.

Each Source
has layers of
opportunity,
and together
they unfold to
reveal its shape.

TECHNOLOGY

EXPRESSION

BUSINESS MODEL

ORGANIZATION

ENVIRONMENT

MARKET

SIX SOURCES MARKET

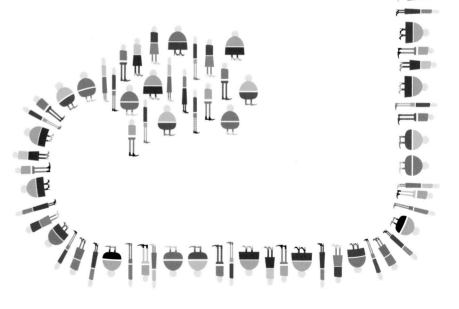

The market is the collective of our customers, distribution, and retailers. Complex and constantly evolving, it is a continual Source of new opportunity. From the emergence of a middle class in developing countries to the aging of populations in developed countries, shifts in buying power change what people want across almost every product category.

Approximately 60% of China's population was born after China's one child policy was instituted in 1979, meaning that many of them grew up as only children. Called "Little Emperors" both in and out of China, they are acculturated toward relatively instant gratification and conspicuous consumption. Combine those traits with rising income in the nation and you have a meteoric rise of a consumer culture driving demand for everything from cars to cosmetics.

Alternatively, not all demand is conspicuous. Markets' needs are often less than obvious, concealed even from consumers themselves. Unseen beneath the surface, these needs promise new opportunity.

Automobile companies have been perfecting observation and design skills, expanding opportunity through new features such as the first cup holder, heated seats, DVD players in minivans, Wi-Fi, and hands-free navigation. New features such as these often meet unarticulated needs.

Opportunity from the market emerges as we sell products where and how consumers want us to sell them. Retail channels have evolved from boutique to mass, from bricks and mortar to online. With people on the go, vending has seen a resurgence. You can snack on a live Shanghai hairy crab in Nanjing, China, a baguette in France, or fresh French fries in Canada. You can purchase farm fresh eggs in Japan, pick up live worms for fishing in Poland, a bicycle in the Netherlands, new jeans in Italy, or ballet flats for tired feet while clubbing in London. You can even secure gold-to-go in Germany for the next financial crisis.

Our markers are
a moving target of
needs, wants, and
desires that come in
all shapes and sizes
and spur opportunity.

Industrial goods companies are also tailoring how they meet customers' needs. E-commerce in business-to-business was initially used by plastics companies to move excess inventory. It has since become a way to offer customers with low technical needs a lower priced product, while selling higher service and higher priced offers to those who want them.

Much like the Russian Matryoshka nesting dolls, markets exist as segments within segments. We can group people along the lines of demographics, attitudes, lifestyles, or the benefits they seek. Opportunity reveals itself when we look at the same market through a different lens.

Traditional car-rental services provide temporary transportation during repairs or travel. Zipcar noticed a need among urbanites and college students with little space, money, or desire for their own cars. They built a car-sharing company that rents cars by the hour with pick up and drop off in spaces throughout cities and universities in the UK, Canada, Spain, and the United States. Their insight led to a 328% growth in three years.

SIX SOURCES TECHNOLOGY

Technology is the backbone of what we sell. Spurred by our inventive spirit, it is a catalyst of opportunity. Technology broadly refers to what we make and the know-how behind it. It is the food in the package, the goo in the bottle, the packaging materials, the shelf it sits on, and the infrastructure of the store in which it is purchased.

Every improvement in a product, service, or process—be it in usability, cost, or efficiency—is a technological advance.

A German appliance company, Miele, has been innovating for over 100 years to make tasks easier—starting with a butter churn and evolving to today's high-end appliances. They boast one of the world's most sophisticated and expensive dishwashers with a double waterproof system, quiet operations, concealed control panel, and 16 different wash programs that can be updated via your PC or tablet.

On the other side of Europe you can find an ingenious low-tech solution. In Belarus a kitchen cabinet above the sink might have a dish rack in its base so dishes can drip dry, saving labor and counter space.

While markets evolve, technology accelerates. Once started, technology picks up further momentum with a force like a snowball rolling down a hill, eventually creating an avalanche of change.

The film industry is a moving picture of the breadth of opportunity stemming from technology. Spurred by the development of the camera and film, it grew in every

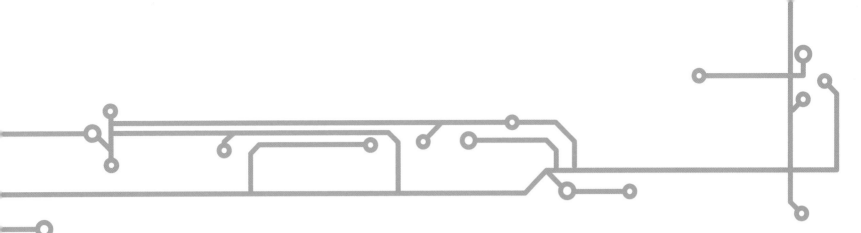

direction. Filming advanced from 10 to 16, 24, 48, and 60 frames per second. Sound came out of an entirely different field, but overtook the stage in just three years. Special effects, computer animation, and 3-D drew in digital technology. Animation has moved from clay to anime. While few patents have been issued, artists have created sophisticated techniques in filming, acting, and editing. We once watched these wonders as a pianist accompanied the film; now the seats themselves can vibrate and blow smoke. From the early nickelodeon, to theaters, drive-ins, iMax, and home theaters with VCRs, and then to projectors and streaming, both architecture and consumer electronics have made contributions. And let's not forget the popcorn! Mr. C. Cretors' invention in 1893 enabled popcorn to be popped inside a building rather than out on the street, and the firm is still busy popping today!

Technology can go unobserved by our customers, used behind the scenes to refine and perfect how we do what we do.

Italian race car maker Ferrari partnered with AMD chip maker to create what may be the real hero in the car: a host of sensors and data-crunching analytics. More than 150 sensors open up over 2,500 telemetry channels enabling better design and driving. From digital wind tunnels to real-time car and track feedback on lateral G-forces, lift, temperature, and more, the two firms have created a crucial ingredient to engineering success. Ferrari has the most victories in Formula 1 history because they have stayed on the leading edge of new technology.

New ways to solve problems stretch our opportunities.

SIX SOURCES ORGANIZATION

Our organization is the who and how of the value we create. While markets drive what we produce, within our own walls we are the masters of how we produce. This autonomy makes the organization a comfortable place to look for opportunity, taking the view of, "Let's start with what we do now." Cost reduction and process improvement often add to the bottom line more reliably than new products. The insights for these improvements frequently come from our own people.

Our people are our greatest asset—if we just knew what they did! So let's ask them! New programs seeking suggestions on how to save money are driving millions to the bottom line. An American Airlines pilot suggested refueling at each stopover so planes carried less fuel. Along with other weight-reduction strategies, this resulted in savings of $141 million in one year alone.

How we organize ourselves can translate into improved service, faster delivery, and higher quality, in turn delighting customers.

Amazon incurred a large up-front cost by building 18 distribution centers in order to deliver product overnight at lower costs. They started Amazon Prime, which allows customers to pay a flat rate for shipping for a year, driving loyalty and significantly increasing sales. The move has reinvigorated thinking about Amazon's threat to brick-and-mortar stores.

Our organizations are the opportunity engines of growth.

Our growth potential improves as we learn better how to organize our efforts for capturing opportunity itself.

The Industrial Research Institute, started over 75 years ago, is one of the leading organizations for research and development (R+D) leaders. This strength is due in part to their Research on Research model. Members study and implement learning on how to manage science to create breakthrough, discover unarticulated needs, incorporate design, and track the future of R+D itself. Their findings are changing how companies organize for opportunity.

Opportunity expands further when the people of opportunity meet. The people of opportunity include those in our organizations, markets, and environments. Companies are learning that in order to serve markets far from their homes they need to immerse themselves in the cultures they hope to serve. Toyota was one of the first to do this on a large scale.

They Act Global Think Local, adapting cars to local driving conditions and tastes.

Companies are finding new ways to organize to capture parts of opportunities that seem out of reach due to cost constraints. Frugal or Lean innovation is an approach that minimizes development and production resources.

A shining example is the crowd-sourcing of drug R+D efforts, which has resulted in new hope for curing tuberculosis. Frugal innovation has led to using cell phones to replace Automated Teller Machines (ATM) in Africa. Companies with large innovation functions are now seeking to learn how to restructure to become more efficient and agile.

Our business model defines how we make money. It encompasses our basic business structure from for-profit to not-for-profit, public to private, and so on.

Koch Industries is a fascinating growth story. Founded in 1940, they are now one of the largest privately held companies at more than $100 billion in revenue. They have grown through acquisition of complementary companies in industries such as oil, paper, and agriculture, and then by stressing individual accountability and business rigor through their home-grown Market-Based Management method and metrics.

Business model also governs the way we do business, which reflects what we value and how we value what we do.

Technology firms could protect their patents to drive higher prices or make money from licensing them. Food makers could sell under their brands or also through private label store brands. Computer firms can make tech support part of a purchase or charge for it separately.

A more subtle aspect of our business model is how we measure ourselves and our success, sometimes radically changing outcomes for consumers! A fried chicken chain measured the amount of chicken left at the end of the day, inadvertently making customers wait for what seemed like forever for a fresh batch. When they changed the metric to measuring how long people had to wait, consumers got cold chicken that had been fried in advance and was no longer crispy. Our metrics reveal what we value and can unexpectedly change what we deliver to consumers. We need to create metrics that will delight consumers—ones that will deliver hot chicken on time!

Different business models can be used to sell the same product. Who knew there were so many ways to sell air! Companies such as Air Products, Praxair, and Air Liquide sell industrial gases in tanker truckloads to companies and in canisters for breathing to consumers. They even colocate with oil and steel companies, selling directly through pipelines from plants built side by side.

Creative business models can unlock new value for consumers.

Piramal Water started as a charitable initiative addressing the huge challenge of a lack of drinking water for over 720 million people in India. Its founders realized they could have a bigger impact if they turned it into a for-profit business. They started a franchise where people pay 50,000 rupees (about $1,000) and a portion of their revenue to sell water for a fraction of what larger companies charge. They have grown to over 150 franchises across seven states in India. Piramal has also installed 17 water ATMs where consumers can get water with prepaid water cards.

Not-for-profits play with their business model to include both how they gather and give support. Funds can be raised from donations to dues, sponsorships to partnerships, bake sales to government grants. They may be distributed by giving away goods and services, or through microloans and sweat equity.

Kiva eliminates poverty one loan at a time. Individuals with low income get loans to support starting or growing a business by telling their stories online. Donors, or loaners in this case, choose who they want to support and loan $25 and up. In just seven years people in 69 countries have received over $446 million from 948,000 contributors. Kiva's 99% repayment rate means money can be loaned again and again.

Even governments create opportunity from new business models. When the residents of Berkshire, Massachusetts, faced a stagnating local economy they created their own currency! People receive 100 BerkShares for $95 and use the shares to buy goods from local businesses. BerkShares are used to shop for everything from groceries to clothing, facials to limousine rentals. The model reinvigorated the economy with over one million BerkShares circulated in the first nine months and over 3.3 million in six years.

SIX SOURCES EXPRESSION

Expression is how we communicate who we are to the world—it's our brand, positioning, messaging, tone of voice, and design aesthetic. Through it we create emotional engagement far beyond that of any of the other Six Sources, resulting in extreme loyalty and revenue.

Sometimes our brands themselves create value. Licensing of brands accounts for over $187 billion in revenues worldwide. From Disney to the BBC, Sunkist fruit growers to Jim Beam spirits, NASCAR to Kawasaki, companies license their brands to extend them into new markets and product ranges or simply to don everything from key chains to clothing. Revenues can be significant: pro sports teams earn more from licensing their brands than from ticket sales.

Extreme customer loyalty is seen when people get tattooed with their favorite company's logo, from Harley Davidson to Apple, or make it their last wish, as when farmers are buried in a casket prominently displaying the John Deere logo.

Sometimes a logo can become a product itself. Imagine making over $5 billion a year from a picture of a cat. Japanese firm Sanrio has turned Hello Kitty into a global celebrity. You can catch a glimpse of her on an Airbus plane, Fender guitar, a Taiwanese maternity hospital, and Spain's Zara fashion clothing. She has dressed up like KISS and been turned into a dress by Lady Gaga.

Each detail of our expression makes or breaks our image across every touch point with the consumer.

Top hotels perfect their expression in every detail. The Çira an Palace Kempinski, Istanbul, uses period furniture and opulent chandeliers; the Hotel Martinez in Cannes, France, has perfected their art deco decor; and the Burj Al Arab, Dubai, has mastered pure decadence. From the soap dish to helicopter pads, every detail expresses the brand, allowing them to charge up to $30,000 a night for their top suites.

Expression is not just a playground for consumer products. Business-to-business companies are learning to better communicate and monetize their brands. Intel went from a second-tier chip maker to the leader when they launched a $100 million Intel Inside campaign. Their market capitalization went from $10 billion to $200 billion in seven years. Listed as one of the most valuable brands in the world, it is worth over $35 billion.

Repositioning can shift perceptions of not only a company but an entire product category. Pork, in the United States, was a distant third choice after beef and chicken, because it was seen as lower quality and less healthy. In 1987 the National Pork Board radically repositioned it with the campaign, The Other White Meat. The campaign spotlighted little known facts, such as the comparable fat content to chicken and the juiciness shared with beef. Pork sales increased 20% during four years as health-conscious consumers opened their minds and mouths to how tasty pork could be.

Our design and brand is our voice—it both whispers and shouts who we are.

SIX SOURCES ENVIRONMENT

Our environment is everything around us. It includes the forces of governments, regulations, education, the economy, culture, and the media as well as individual influencers such as opinion leaders, celebrities, activists, and bloggers. The influences of one to many and many to one cascades across each of the other Sources creating a multitude of tipping points.

The economy has been seen as the grim reaper of opportunity in recent years, but has actually opened unexpected doors of opportunity. People have been eating out less creating a resurgence in home cooking—opening the door for new shows and gourmet food products and appliances. At the other end of the spectrum, there has been an explosion of super discount dollar stores that are now carrying many food products and a return to Iceland (not the country!), the frozen food store in the UK.

The forces within the environment are often at odds, pushing and shoving for dominance. A third of individuals in the world have Internet access and it's growing every year. Social media usage is at its highest in unexpected places—the Philippines, Russia, and Brazil. At the same time China, the Middle East,

Cuba, Russia, and others are cracking down on its usage. These forces are clashing in ways that will dramatically affect how we tell our stories and sell our wares.

The future of intellectual property (IP)—which has been at the heart of capitalizing on opportunity—may be less in the domain of the technology and business model Sources and more in the hands of the people.

Crowd and open-sourcing approaches are indicators that the world may be moving away from a model of control to one of engagement. Funding models for scientific exploration are becoming more open as well. Yet most companies still require a guarantee that they can protect and monetize their investment in R+D. As a result, countries such as China, long considered to be a threat to IP, are trying to strengthen their laws in order to encourage innovation from within as well as outside.

The resources we use to fuel opportunity are themselves creating opportunity.

Our natural resources are shifting. The energy industry is rapidly changing with new reserves of oil being found in the United States, natural gas in Russia, and new ways to leverage wind, waves, and sunlight all over the world.

Our primary resource for opportunity—people—is also in flux.

People are on the move, migrating more than ever, leading to new opportunities in housing, urban development, and consumer tastes. Yet in many countries, more than half of the talents that could spur opportunity growth are going untapped. Women have limited access to education in over 70 countries, and they make up a disproportionate percent of the impoverished—70%.

While opportunity used to reside largely in the hands of companies, it is becoming more a collaboration with consumers as the world becomes increasingly connected.

In the rise of TOMS Shoes, a culture has rallied around a simple idea. TOMS Shoes was founded by Blake Mycoskie after he witnessed a need for shoes in impoverished populations. For every purchase of a pair of shoes, a pair is donated to someone in need. The model has gained a tidal wave of popular momentum with thousands of people posting pictures of their shoes on Facebook. More than two million shoes have been given to children in over 51 countries. The phenomenon has become a model for other organizations, creating opportunity in its wake.

Influence in the environment tips like dominoes, creating an unstoppable cascade of opportunity.

OPPORTUNITY THINKING

Opportunity thinking goes beyond innovation driven by the market, technologies, new business models or design thinking—to look at all of the Sources of growth.

The definition of opportunity calls for a more holistic view of its Sources.

We can both discover and create opportunity through the Six Sources.

BIG
RELATIONSHIPS

So who got the ball rolling on all the opportunity of the 1400s and beyond? One family stands at the center of influence early in the Age of Exploration and Discovery. In the town of Florence, Italy, in the 1300s, the Medici family was busy laying the groundwork. They were merchants growing a healthy textile business; so healthy that in 1397 they started their own bank—the Medici Bank—from which they bankrolled many an expedition. Of course, a good bank needs good accounting, and they had an exciting breakthrough. Double entry bookkeeping! Perhaps that isn't the most breathtaking invention of all time, but it paved the way for growth of business itself, which in turn funded even more advances.

They supported artists and scientists including Michelangelo, Leonardo da Vinci, Raphael, and Botticelli. They hired Galileo to tutor their children, enabling him to map the universe in his spare time. Their children and grandchildren found their way into leadership in politics and the church, influencing the social fabric of what was hot and what was not. Just imagine the conversations at their dinner table! For hundreds of years they connected the dots of opportunity.

The arts, politics, technology, business structures, and reputations were all interconnected. In the history of a single family we see all Six Sources come together, influencing each other, creating cascades of effects, and together expanding opportunity.

relationship

Their family relationships influenced the nature of opportunity. This shouldn't surprise us since opportunity itself lies in relationship. *Ob portu* reminds us that opportunity is the bringing together of the port, the goods, and the conditions that join them. So, by definition, opportunity is about the perfect conditions: when demand meets supply, need meets invention, creativity becomes the cure.

The relationships among the Six Sources are many.
They share . . .

A common core:
a focal point that
becomes the arbiter
of opportunity.

Tensions:
the tug-of-war between what the
markets want and what can and
should be made.

Synergies:
the potential for the Six Sources
to work together to share talents
and create something new.

Connections:
the relationships between the
people of opportunity—across
our own organizations and
the larger ecosystem.

Opportunity Core

An opportunity is only really an opportunity if it has a reason for being, a beneficiary. It's easy to think the primary beneficiary of opportunity is us! Our own organization, employees, and stockholders—the people most hoping for growth. Certainly we are the beneficiaries of the growth we achieve, but we are not the primary beneficiaries of opportunity itself.

THE BENEFICIARIES ARE THE INDIVIDUALS FOR WHOM WE CREATE VALUE. THEY ARE AT THE CORE OF OPPORTUNITY.

For the consumer goods company, the core is the individual consumer. Here opportunity is expanded by being attentive to the needs of individual consumers, tailoring products to appeal to specific users and providing product ranges so there is something for everyone, from shampoo to laptops. For a business-to-business company, it is the customer, the company that buys. In this case opportunity is grown by understanding the specific needs of the companies sold to and solving problems for each decision maker and user of products and services. For the non-government organization (NGO) or not-for-profits, the core is the community. NGOs accelerate adoption of their programs when they look at the unique roles of each individual within a community. While the Six Sources as a whole look at collectives of people in markets, environments, and the organization, the core represents the individual. It reminds us that opportunity resides in a single person and that ultimately that single person is the arbiter of opportunity—deciding its fate.

Each of the Six Sources serves the core in one way or another. A business model may be designed to drive new revenue to the organization, but it must still meet the needs of the customer if it is to succeed. A technology will only succeed if, ultimately, the consumer finds value in it and so on. Opportunity within and across the Six Sources lies in focusing on innovating not *from* our core but *for* our core constituent.

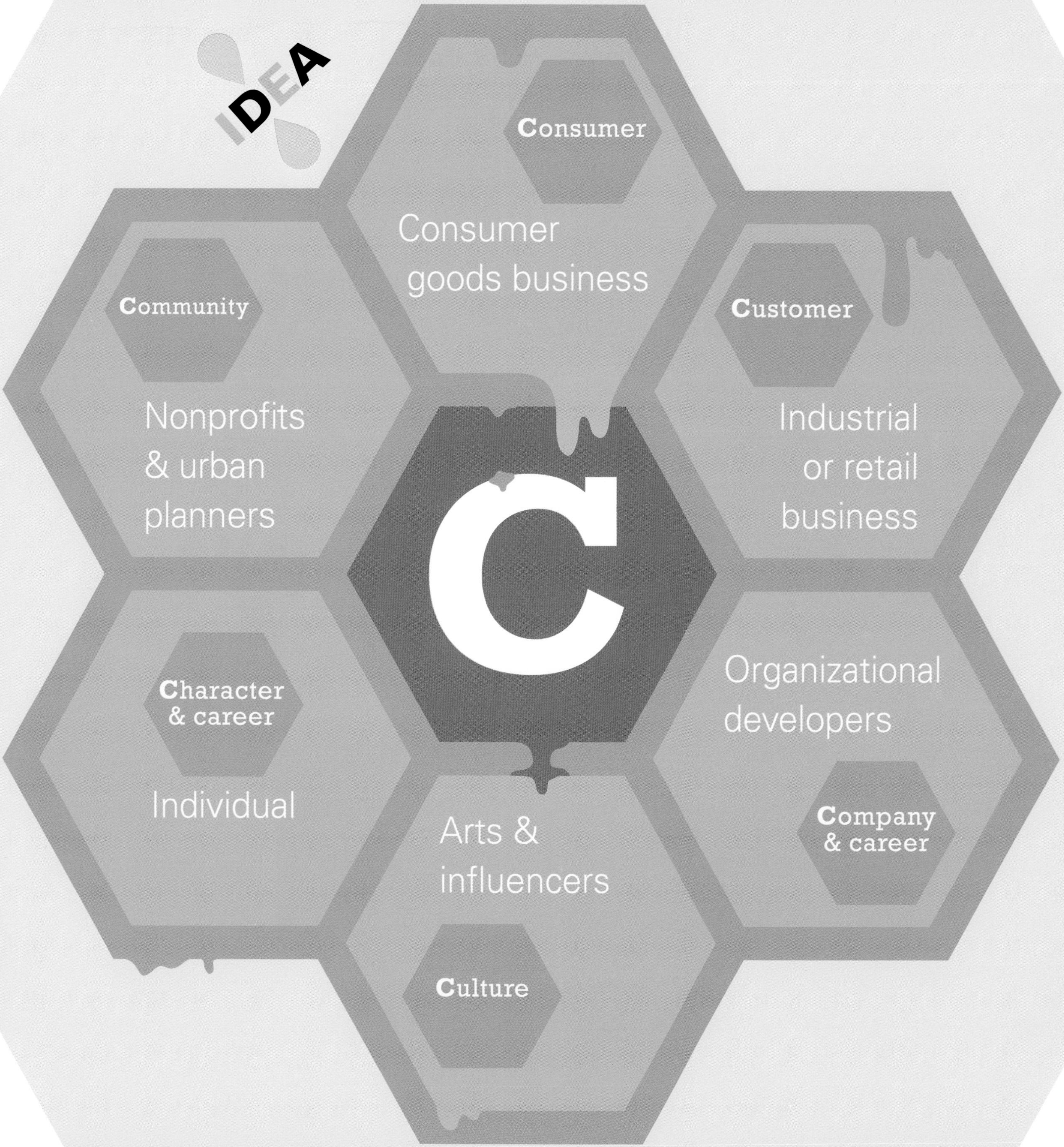

IDEA

Consumer

Consumer
goods business

Community

Nonprofits
& urban
planners

Customer

Industrial
or retail
business

C

Character
& career

Individual

Organizational
developers

Arts &
influencers

Company
& career

Culture

Opportunity Tensions

Just as the Six Sources are all connected to the core, they are also connected to each other. They are bound elastically. Some Sources tend to exert push influence while others are more likely to create pull. The Sources on the top of our diagram—technology, expression, and business model—make up the bulk of what we offer and create what we push. The Sources on the bottom —market, environment, and organization—all represent collectives of people and exert pull for what is created.

For Sources to push the creation and growth of opportunity, they will need a heavy dose of anticipation of the potential pull from our markets, environments, and organizations. For pull to germinate opportunity it must synchronize with a push of invention and creativity from new technologies, expressions, and business models. A dynamic system of push and pull between the Sources reveals the creative tensions for growth. Although each Source can and should be mined for opportunity individually, the tensions between them are at the heart of the definition of opportunity. While they all interact, there exist pairs of Sources that tend to fit together in a yin-yang of opposing forces.

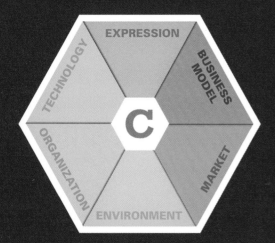

Technology push—Market pull

Technology push versus market pull is a well-known tension, often a source of debate about how to achieve growth. Some people insist that greater opportunity lies in one or the other. It is their marriage, though, that leads to opportunity; together, they create a compounding cycle of impact. A new technology is of no value if the market doesn't want it, but it is sometimes difficult to say what the market will accept—a new technology can be a game-changer and awaken realization of unarticulated needs. Conversely, markets with articulated needs drive organizations to develop new technology to meet those needs, and those technologies then lead to platforms that can be pushed into new markets. Like a flywheel, the movement builds up momentum and creates ever more change.

> "Wise men make more opportunity than they find."

Francis Bacon, philosopher, scientist, statesman

The push and pull of technology and markets is seen in almost every industry. It may be more obvious in the evolution of big technologies such as electricity, the Internet, or computer chips; however, such forces occur anywhere there are market-driven advances in technology.

🌳 The market for sweetening food expanded from honey to sugar to corn syrup. With increased weight concerns, consumers wanted low calorie sweeteners, leading to the development of Sweet'N Low, NutraSweet, and Splenda. These artificial sweeteners then expanded the market for diet foods, spurring hundreds of new food and beverage products. But the market is changing and is now demanding more natural alternatives, such as Maltitol found in vegetables, Sorbitol from plums, Xylitol from oats, Isomalt from beet roots, Erythritol found in pears, and brands such as Stevia from a South American shrub and Agave nectar from a plant found in Mexico. 🌳

Every industry grows through the push of invention and the pull of market demand, leading to new opportunities.

Business Model push—Organizational pull

This push and pull tension also exists between business models and organizations. Organizations often look for new business models to drive margin increases and revenue expansion. Business model innovations are designed to push that new value to the organization. But the new business model also pushes and sometimes shoves an organization to make radical changes in how it delivers that value, demanding that the organization learn new skills in delivering, for example, services rather than products, selling value instead of volume. Often the antibodies of internal resistance come out and reject the change as too foreign to business-as-usual. Sometimes the transition is too difficult and the organization fails to make the leap.

🌳 It was Amazon, not Barnes & Noble or Borders, that succeeded first at online book sales. It was late entrants Japanese Sony and Nikon, and ultimately phone manufacturers Motorola and Nokia, not Kodak or Polaroid, who made digital photography business models replace the model of monetizing film.🌳

Organizations that successfully adopt new business models often lead transformation of an entire industry.

The push and pull tension is a yin-yang relationship that governs opportunity potential.

Expression push—Environment pull

A third tension shows up in the push and pull between our expression and the environment. Our brands and design aesthetics can change culture as well as be inspired by it. It is the same creative question that arises around whether art creates culture or culture inspires art. Our expression is something we push to communicate to the marketplace, the environment, and our own employees, while the wider culture pulls us to adapt and shape what we say about ourselves. The environment acts as the audience, interpreter, advocate, and judge of our messages, and so its influence can create new opportunities for expression.

🌳 Nike has a strong brand name built through constant dialogue. When Nike was saddled with concerns over sweat-shop labor and again when its footwear became gang fashion, the company changed its practices. They used hand-picked spokespeople—first athletes whose ranks included Michael Jordan and Serena Williams, and celebrities such as Spike Lee, and eventually events such as the World Cup—to reflect new positioning through the voices of the environment itself. The environment shaped Nike's expression. Conversely, Nike's expression has also shaped the environment. The slogan, "Just do it" has become part of the vernacular of the culture leading to its use in book titles, TV show episodes, and rap music lyrics.🌳

Leveraging the push and pull between Sources creates bigger opportunities. It compounds what we can do in one Source, stretching it, and ensuring greater success.

Opportunity Synergies

While there are tensions across the opposing forces, there are synergies between the neighbors. The neighboring Sources share much in common.

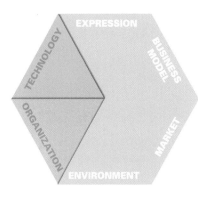

The organization supports the infrastructure of technology, building capabilities, assets, and protecting IP, while technology reciprocates by feeding the organization with process improvements and revenue potential.

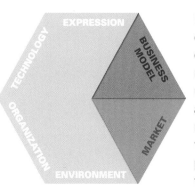

Business model and market combine to create the classic supply and demand relationship. As price goes up, demand goes down, and vice versa. The business model is informed by what the market will bear, while pushing to capture more of the market potential.

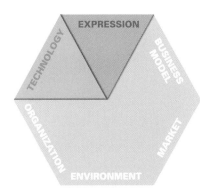

Technology and expression share the design function: creating usability and the aesthetics of product, experience, and packaging design as well as the imagery of graphic design and brand identity. Design itself is both a technical and expressive field.

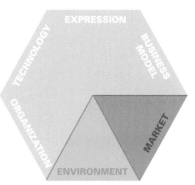

The market sits within the larger environment but also influences it. Market is defined, in part, by culture and the dynamics of economy and regulation in the environment but it can also be the originator and driver of these macro influences.

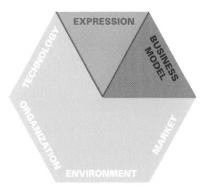

Expression and business model shape the positioning of products and services to the market. Expression creates brands that demand higher prices, while the business model determines both price points and the investment levels in the brand.

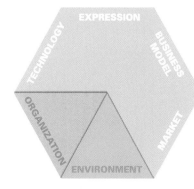

The organization sits within the environment, accessing its natural and human resources. The environment creates the legal and cultural guardrails for business operation. The commercial organization then feeds the economy, providing a tax base for governments and, ideally, restoring the environment through its triple bottom line.

Opportunity Influences

While all Six Sources have a role to play in opportunity, they aren't all weighted equally in every situation. Some will be more applicable depending on the nature of the business or function. Technology companies will be drawn to focus on R+D, banks on their business model, retailers on their markets, etc. Our capabilities make us more suited for gaining growth from one Source over another, but growth won't always reside in the obvious places. New opportunities may be germinated where we least expect them and therefore where few of our competitors have bothered looking.

🌳 A coffee company could continue to perfect their roast, but Starbucks found opportunity in creating the third place, the place you go other than work and home, exacting growth from the environment, business model, and expression.

Grocery stores long looked almost solely to their suppliers and customers for opportunity but have found growth through new business models and online sales that enable delivery services.

Companies that long gained revenue from their technologies, product development, and markets found growth in a new business model—leasing. Power-by-the-Hour was perfected by Rolls Royce. They provide engines for airplanes and charge for maintenance and parts, allowing the airplane operator to stop managing maintenance, maintain fixed costs for upkeep and parts, and instead focus attention on finding growth opportunities. Leasing is unlocking revenue for all kinds of equipment companies pursuing growth in developing markets where the up-front costs are too high and people prefer to pay as they go. 🌳

EXPRESSION

BUSINESS MODEL

TECHNOLOGY

ORGANIZATION

MARKET

ENVIRONMENT

A picture of ourselves

Each of the Sources represents not only a fountainhead of opportunity, but also the people within our organization who create and capture opportunity. From R+D to brand, finance to marketing, public affairs to operations, we each have a role to play in opportunity. Our jobs are to explore opportunity within our own functions. R+D develops technology, marketing looks at needs and segments in the market, brand managers drive our expression, financial analysts enhance the business model, engineering improves operations, and legal covers our flanks. Opportunity increases as we each do our part. But opportunity is even greater as all the pieces come together. When it comes to opportunity, the whole is greater than the sum of the parts.

The push and pull between the Sources, their synergies, and their common purpose in the core creates the biggest opportunity of all. Opportunity presents itself not only in the Six Sources, but also in their interaction. Yet sometimes the Sources interact more than we do!

Capturing opportunity demands that we interact with the same intensity and coordination, anticipation and invention as the Sources themselves. It is in these interactions that we are most likely to harness big opportunity.

Unfortunately many organizations are simply not set up to interact with each other. They are driven by operational excellence within their functions and struggle to figure out how to cross the hall to collaborate.

Our organizations look nothing like the world of opportunity.

Opportunity emerges and is satisfied when the Six Sources come together. When our organizations fail to model these interactions, instead hiding in their own functions, we risk missing opportunity and creating offers that are mismatched with desire.

To illustrate the importance of cross functionality, just imagine we are in a traditionally siloed company and we set out to do something extraordinary. We endeavor to create a bird! What might our process look like? Divide and conquer! R+D and engineering discover and design the ideal wing mechanism for perfect flight. Supply chain works out the best possible beak to collect food. The IT team gives it the smartest of bird brains. Plumage and song fall to the brand and marketing teams, and the operations team comes up with the best nest-building instinct. Each function goes off on its own and designs the very best bit of bird anatomy imaginable. But when we pull all the pieces together to create the ideal bird, chances are it wouldn't fly, and doubtless it wouldn't last five minutes before a predator ate it.

When product offers are similarly designed with hand-offs between functions it's no wonder many don't fly—or even survive—after launch. So, too, it is with looking for opportunity. We look at the parts and not the whole and in doing so fail to get off the ground.

A view of the world

The need for collaboration isn't limited to inside the company. The Six Source functional groups of people within the organization are just a microcosm of the wider world of technologists, designers, financiers, manufacturers, and marketers who influence our opportunities and make up the overall opportunity ecosystem.

Within this ecosystem also sit our competitors, each of whom can be described according to their Six Sources. Competitors influence us across all of the Sources. They race to create and protect technologies. They build brands that influence culture and markets, and create messages that compete for the airwaves. Their business models vie for dominance, and their organizations compete for talent. They jostle for shelf space, cupboard space, and space in the minds and hearts of our consumers.

Each opportunity ecosystem is unique.

Beyond our competition there is a world bursting with people creatively pushing the boundaries of both what can be done and what might be wanted. The opportunity ecosystem is made up of people and groups who influence, observe, or participate in an opportunity. Each opportunity ecosystem is unique—it is not the entire world but all those who are engaged in an opportunity, which could be quite a large group indeed.

While we may choose to ignore those in the opportunity ecosystem, our consumers will not. They will be affected by the opinions and inventions that emerge, now more than ever as the world becomes increasingly connected.

🌳 Vertu is the luxury phone company started in 1998 in the UK by Finnish firm Nokia. Responsible for creating and producing the most expensive handsets in the world—diamond- and jewel-encrusted designs costing between £3,500 and £213,000 (about $5,400–$333,500)—they have avoided traditional channels. From the beginning they tightly defined their opportunity ecosystem and purposely put it to work for them. They started out by giving their handsets to celebrities, relying on their social circles and the paparazzi to spread the word. Partnering with Ferrari and French watch and jewelry designer Boucheron further defined their brand and their customer base. They worked with exclusive service providers in Dubai, Moscow, Milan, Tokyo, Beijing, Hong Kong, Mumbai, Los Angeles, New York, and London to provide personal concierge services. Establishments such as Berry Bros and Rudd, Britain's oldest wine and spirits merchant, offered Vertu owners first refusal on rare and collectible vintages. All together Vertu created opportunity hand in hand with the ecosystem. 🌳

The opportunity ecosystem is a kaleidoscope of overlapping ecosystems.

Living deeply enmeshed in it, looking to it for insight, and drawing members into meaningful interaction brings richer perspective to bear on opportunity and ultimately expands it further.

Open innovation and open opportunities

The opportunity ecosystem defines the depth and breadth of connections available to us. An organization that looks externally as well as internally will discover untold possibilities. In recent years this has become evident as more and more companies explore open innovation in seeking technology inputs from outside companies. They have realized that no matter how well they play the talent game, not all the smart people work for them.

Looking at open innovation through the eyes of opportunity builds on this momentum and greatly expands potential. While much of the focus has been on generating new ideas within R+D, we need not limit our openness to R+D nor to ideas only. Understanding the breadth of the ecosystem expands our potential openness across all Six Sources and moves us from idea creation to opportunity development. People in every function of our companies can practice some form of openness. They can do so both to generate new ideas and to expand their opportunities. After all, opportunity is created through relationships, and when we connect with others we expand both our pool of relationships, and our opportunities. We move beyond practicing open innovation to practicing open opportunity!

Opening efforts to explore and create opportunity to include those in other companies can start within each of the functions. This has been happening for years through the informal relationships that occur in trade associations. More formally, we see companies engaging in consortium to share best practices. Openness has occurred when people have come together to share their Lean or sustainability practices. Organizations that band together to self-regulate are innovating to improve their industry as well as keep at bay government bodies.

A long list of companies across the food industry, such as PepsiCo, ConAgra, Mars, and Campbell's Soup, have joined together to self-regulate their advertising to children, committing to maintain more than 50% of their ads to children focused on healthy choices.

Designers work with other designers sharing insights on new materials; partnerships are formed to go after bigger opportunities; products are co-branded in order to expand reputation in new ways. All of these efforts stretch opportunity for the participants as well as for those who follow in their footsteps.

Relationships beget relationships.

Open opportunity and open innovation are expanded further when people join forces across the functions.

Organization + Environment

People Tree is a fashion company based in the UK that features unique pieces hand-stamped by women who have started small businesses in developing nations. The proceeds are greater when selling these pieces through People Tree's global distribution networks than the women would normally receive. By opening up their organization to employing and partnering with people all over the world, People Tree has created new value for consumers and expanded opportunity for a better standard of living in developing nations, which further spurs opportunity for others. Practicing open opportunity before open innovation will increase the odds of success.

Brands + Consumers

Brands benefit from greater openness with their consumers. Through ongoing contests for photo submissions, as well as collecting ideas through their custom bottle-design tool on their website, Jones Soda taps the rich imagination of the ecosystem to develop a label aesthetic now called iconic.

Technology + Environment + Consumers

Inventors have traditionally looked for funding from government, companies, or venture capitalists, but a new generation of garage inventors is receiving funding and feedback from interested people through crowd-funding. Funding site Kickstarter has channeled over $500 million to more than 3 million people for in excess of 35,000 projects. Social product development company Quirky attracts funding and insight and then helps market the products on their site and through more than 188 retail partners. More than 350 new products have been launched, each listing the inventor and the number of people who contributed thoughts. Almost 400,000

inventive collaborators participate, and new products are launched at a rate of two per week.

Design + Technology + Market

GE Plastics started a movement in industrial goods when they joint ventured with Fitch, one of the world's largest design firms. They used design to inspire new thinking on what was possible with their materials; in doing so they expanded opportunity, selling more material. Since then German companies Bayer Materials Sciences and BASF, Dutch firm DSM, U.S. textile and chemical company Milliken, aluminum firm Novelis, and others have all developed design centers.

Business Model + Environment

Community water purification projects in developing nations have often failed because of a lack of operating funds. Waterlife is a new company that has formed a public–private partnership in which they run the plants for the government in India and charge a user fee from customers. They now run over 2,000 plants and are growing at over 300% per year.

Like turning a kaleidoscope, the potential creative outcomes of overlapping connections are endless.

While many of these examples are big ideas, even killer ideas, they each expand the underlying opportunity. The ideas are so big they leave in their wake opportunity for others—new ways of doing things, new partners, new thinking across the opportunity ecosystem. Opportunity is expanded through the openness of the organization to others. Practicing open opportunity before open innovation will increase the odds of success.

It takes a culture to define a culture-changing opportunity.

A holistic picture of opportunity

As we pursue growth through the Six Sources, we see that opportunity can be expanded through actions within one single Source, but a single Source alone is not where a complete opportunity lies.

Opportunity can be focused and refined through connection to the core, stretched through the give-and-take of anticipation and invention found in the push and pull tensions, enriched through the relationships between neighboring Sources, and opened up beyond our own isolated imagination when we open ourselves to our colleagues and the broader opportunity ecosystem.

A hot opportunity

Consider a growing opportunity . . . appliances! Sound a bit dull? Not to the over 3 billion people who don't have a safe stove, let alone a refrigerator, washing machine, or dishwasher. The need goes beyond the convenience factor. Over 1.9 million people die each year from fumes from cooking fires, making it the fourth largest cause of death in developing nations. Add to this tragedy the impact on the environment: a cooking fire produces as much CO_2 as a car and leads to deforestation. The opportunity is significant and many are taking notice. Inventors are congregating to design new solutions. Stovecamp in Oregon is attracting collectives of designers who strive to create a stove that will last five years, cook an array of foods, burn wood cleanly with little smoke, and cost only $10. Envirofit.org has launched a range of stoves tailored to the unique cooking and fuel needs of different consumers. In partnership with Shell Oil's Foundation, they have developed innovative distribution channels that involve local people, NGOs, and governments throughout Africa and India. They are partnering now with C-Quest Finance, a carbon finance organization, to sell stoves in Latin America and Africa. Through an innovative business model, C-Quest covers the costs of the stoves and recoups the money by selling the carbon credits coming from the large amount of CO_2 reduced by each stove each year! The model works because of new guidelines from the UN on carbon credits.

The opportunity for appliances doesn't stop with stoves or with the impoverished. China's Haier has become the world's largest white goods company by designing right-sized appliances for both developing and developed nations. For the higher end of the market, Hisense, also from China, is incorporating Android applications to control appliances.

The opportunity ecosystem is brimming with all the tell-tale signs of big growth potential. There remain significant unmet needs for appliances and novel approaches to meeting those needs through new business models, technologies, brands, and new ways to organize and partner.

The need for appliances may long have existed, but this new shape of opportunity today is the result of changes in access, business models, culture, laws, and awareness. The coming together of many forces is what drives opportunity. This is the picture of our port, goods, and the timing of the tides and winds—an image recognized and written about long ago by Shakespeare and an image equally applicable to our endeavors.

> "There is a tide in the affairs of men.
> Which, taken at the flood, leads on to fortune;
> Omitted, all the voyage of their life
> Is bound in shallows and in miseries.
> On such a full sea are we now afloat,
> And we must take the current when it serves,
> Or lose our ventures."
>
> *Brutus, Julius Caesar,*
> *Act IV. scene 3, 218–224*
> *William Shakespeare*

OPPORTUNITY THINKING

Opportunity resides in relationships. Maximize our relationships and we maximize our opportunities.

The ecosystem includes those who observe, influence, and participate in opportunity.

It invites us to explore open opportunity before open innovation.

WE ARE EACH ACTIVE PARTICIPANTS IN OPPORTUNITY.

CHAPTER 4

BIG

EXPLORATION

⛴ The Age of Exploration was not just one of ships and sails, spices and silk. It was an Age of Information. Traveling long distances created a need for new kinds of information, and that spurred a technological revolution. Explorers were the original Techies during this boom. They sought out the latest gadgets and devices. They quickly learned how to see farther, snapping up new telescopes; think more spatially, investing in the latest sextants, quadrants, marine astrolabes, and the first globes; and imagine in greater color and detail as they read, recorded, and published accounts via the newly invented printing press.

Printing presses not only cranked out reports of new lands, they produced volumes on the science and art of discovery and navigation itself. People were discovering the methodologies for exploration. Pedro de Medina's *Arte de Navegar*, published in 1545, was translated into French, Italian, Dutch, and English. John Davis revealed his secrets in 1594 in the *Seaman's Secrets*. As governments and explorers alike raced for fame and fortune, they did so through a race for understanding—understanding first and foremost how to explore. ⛴

Similarly, we Opportunity Explorers need to up our game—we need the latest methods if we are to discover opportunity. Where is our go-to tool kit that will deliver a clear view of opportunity?

After all, we too need to see beyond the usual limits of our observation in order to know what is on the horizon, what is coming that will spell opportunity for us. Trends are the key. They help us look further.

We also need to see where we are and where we want to go, understand where there is and is not opportunity. Dimensionalizing opportunity is the trick to working out the opportunity landscape.

Finally, we need to see the lands we discover in their full color, recording our discoveries for others so we can get on with capturing opportunity. We do this by uncovering rich insights and bringing along others to discover with us.

> "The real voyage of discovery consists not in seeking new landscapes but in having new eyes."
>
> *Marcel Proust,*
> *French essayist and*
> *cultural critic*

These are the ways we find opportunity. They are our tools of exploration—our three Opportunity Finders. Opportunity trends, dimensions, and insights define the height, width, breadth, and depth of our opportunities. Through these we:

LOOK OUT.
WORK OUT.
FIND OUT.

WE CAN BE DISCIPLINED ABOUT DEFINING OPPORTUNITY.

Three Opportunity Finders are our tool kits for exploring opportunity:

- Opportunity Trends help us
  Look Out to see what is changing.

- Opportunity Dimensions help us
  Work Out the landscape and where to grow.

- Opportunity Insights help us
  Find Out the rich nature of opportunity.

BIG TRENDS

Look Out: Opportunity Trends

⚓ Before the Weather Channel ever hit the airwaves in 1982, there was the Medici Network, started in 1654. It was the first coordinated effort to gather temperature and other weather data such as rainfall, air pressure, evaporation rates, and currents. The network spanned an amazing 11 different regions along the Mediterranean and beyond, across what is today Italy, France, Germany, Austria, and Poland. Weather information was gathered regularly and then consolidated and analyzed. The Network enabled the creation of weather maps that revealed changes in atmospheric pressure over the region and thus the nature of weather systems. By tracking weather patterns and understanding the laws of change, one could know more than a couple of hours ahead if the conditions would be right for sailing into port! ⚓

Climate and sea conditions can prove to be either friend or foe, sometimes helping and sometimes hurting the fortunes of a merchant.

In the same way, change in our world opens and closes the windows of opportunity. Without change we would soon exhaust the opportunities we have. People change, technologies change, cultures change and so opportunities emerge or disappear for new products and services. **Change is like reshuffling a deck. It can turn up just the cards we need or deal us hands we didn't expect.**

It is a paradox that we hate change but we love new things. So to find new opportunities we have to move from bracing for change to embracing change, recognizing that without change opportunity would stagnate, dwindle, or be fully tapped out.

We have to get comfortable, even fluent, in the types of change to watch for, from megatrends to microtrends, cycles to seeds of new things to come. Each helps us look out across the opportunity landscape to see where new opportunity might emerge.

66 The universe is change; our life is what our thoughts make of it. 99

Marcus Aurelius Antonius, Roman emperor and philosopher

Megatrends

Megatrends are the major weather patterns blowing across our opportunity landscape. Their impact cuts across industries and people groups, driven by and driving shifts at a global scale. Megatrends include aging population, resource shortages, climate change, urbanization, and the economic shift toward developing nations. They are major activators of opportunity, impacting myriad communities in the ecosystem, affecting business conditions, consumer markets, and the natural environment.

Often megatrends are already so well established that they can hardly be considered trends anymore. So it wouldn't seem that they would yield new opportunity. Yet they do.

Consider the aging population (which technically includes all of us!).

Today those older than 60 number 817 million.

By 2050 they will number 2 billion.

Of those, 80% will live in what are now developing nations.

Every continent will see an increase of at least 50% in the number of people older than 60.

Globally, this population is considered to be at risk—for housing, care, safety, and nutrition.

But not universally.

In the United States, for example, about 25% of the population is older than 60. But they wield 40% of the United States' spending power, almost $2 trillion a year.

This is what caught some people off guard—the sheer spending power of the segment, alongside their increasingly healthy and youthfully minded lifestyles—creating an ongoing stream of new opportunity.

🌳 Opportunity has abounded across a wide range of industries and regions. Antiaging products have boomed, from Oil of Olay to Botox, antiaging supplements to special vitamin-infused water.

The travel and leisure industry has developed specialty cruises and tours, while the financial industry has developed new investment products. The romance industry has perhaps seen some of the most remarkable growth from online dating services to Viagra. 🌳

Megatrends may often seem worn out, but they cut across so much of the landscape that they provide almost boundless opportunity.

Microtrends

Microtrends, conversely, affect a subset of industries, regions, or people groups. These are like local weather systems that are specific to a region.

Not everyone is aware of or would ever care about the fact that there is a global shortage of helium! The second most abundant element—in every breath we take—is pulled from the air and natural gas and then used for cooling in industries such as computer chip wafer manufacturing, welding, and space exploration.

Microtrends have a way of spilling over into adjacent areas, impacting our lives in unexpected ways. You might have to substitute a piñata for balloons at your next birthday party, or you may have a harder time getting an MRI scan. A shortage of one resource means that innovation must occur elsewhere; as a result medical device companies are busy trying to reduce helium usage in their equipment.

Microtrends also show up in specific regions and people groups. When the megatrend of urbanization meets new attitudes toward fresh, local food, what emerges is a microtrend of urban farming. From rooftop gardens to strawberries being grown in drain pipes and potatoes in dust bins, people are creating ways to grow their own fresh food.

Some microtrends tumble out of a confluence of megatrends. Combine urbanization and the rising costs of materials and we get microhousing that uses a fraction of building material, produces much less waste, and features far more efficient design than traditional housing. Originally based on the cramped conditions in Japan and other high-density population areas, new interest has arisen in, of all places, the United States! Following Hurricane Katrina, 300 square foot Katrina Cottages were created as temporary housing. Their design grabbed attention. High-end, beautifully designed microhousing is being demonstrated in Seattle, New York, San Francisco, and Boston, as well as Barcelona, Manchester, and, of course, Japan.

Both megatrends and microtrends are easily spotted because of their magnitude and impact. We use them as our telescope for looking into the future. We need to look broadly, though, because our own industries, markets, technologies, and resources are not isolated from those adjacent to us.

As with dominoes tipping, once started, they do not stop. The effects will eventually reach us.

Six kinds of change

Change is inevitable—not just in people groups, natural resources, or new technologies—it percolates across all of the Six Sources. We may be accustomed to traditional trends reports that focus on changes in the market, environment, or technology but miss out thinking about trends in business models, brands and design, and organizations.

Business models have been changing rapidly, particularly as companies seek new ways of expanding opportunity in developing markets. Micro and interest-free loans, public and private partnerships, and leasing have seen new applications from Africa to India to South America.

"Become a student of change.
It is the only thing that will remain constant."

Anthony D'Angelo, education author

Trends in expression range from the evolution of brands to the style used in product, package, and brand design. There is a new wave of distrust for big brands and a pendulum swing toward smaller, quirkier brands. Rogue brands are seen in the explosion of craft brews with names like Moose Drool, Smooth Hoperator, Half-life Hefeweizen, and He'brew—The Chosen Beer!

Design aesthetic is on the move, becoming more modern and greener. Andreas Froese, a German engineer and architect of green housing, happened to be helping clean up a park in Honduras when he realized just how many plastic bottles were being thrown away. He started to collect them and soon came up with a way to use them to build homes by combining them with sand and other trash. He established ECOTEC and grew an organization that both builds homes and trains other builders across Latin America, India, and now Africa. Architects and builders alike are experimenting with a broader range of materials including repurposing shipping containers and boats, using old car tires for foundations, and using bottle caps for mosaics.

Across the design world there is a revolution in the use of materials previously discarded. Clothing designer Mizrahi created an ethereal dress of salmon leather using tiny sequins of fish skin. Nike won awards for their Trash Talk shoe made from leather, foam, and rubber that is typically thrown away after making their trainers.

Organizations are also seeing change. With the downturn in the economy they have reduced their staff. An aging workforce is retiring in huge numbers and companies are now finding they must invest more heavily in knowledge management services, software, and infrastructure.

Change occurs across all Six Sources opening new opportunities in potentially unexpected places.

Seeds, cycles, and clashes

While the world is buzzing with megatrends and microtrends across the Six Sources, the change that could create the next opportunity may be too small to be called a trend. Yet, it might be the start of something new.

Like the first snowflake foretells a possible winter wonderland, so the first and almost undetectable glimmer of change in an ecosystem may foretell the next big trend. It might be the creation by a single artist, the ringing voice of a lone, impassioned opinion leader, an invention from an obscure startup, or the exchanges between a few busy bloggers. We call these seed trends—not really trends, but the suggestion of a new direction and the possible seed of a trend to come.

🌳 A viral video on the "Great Pacific Garbage Patch" told the story of plastic products and water bottles gathering in a vortex in the Pacific, a vortex some claim to be the size of Texas. There was then a TEDx event featuring speakers illuminating the origins and implications of the garbage patch. These influences spurred many to reconsider water bottles and other disposable plastics. The ripples are still felt as cities and states cut their budget allocations for bottled water and urge residents to consider alternatives. Some drinking fountains are now being designed to allow for refilling water bottles and display a counter that reports the plastic bottles saved each time a reusable bottle is filled. 🌳

The traces of things to come reveal the spaces for things to come.

Seed trends can also appear in new product introductions—the first product to call out a particular ingredient or attribute. In many cases these products are from smaller companies that can afford to serve niche markets, but markets that won't stay niche for long.

We often see trends as proverbial snowballs, picking up speed and size as they roll down the hill. Taken from a longer view, though, we find that not all trends are quite so one-directional. Some get recycled. They come around time and again like the seasons across our landscape.

Just as seasonal weather cycles vary year-to-year, the cycles of trends have their own idiosyncrasies.

Fashions repeat, the economy cycles, political topics return to vogue, and pendulums swing in organizational approaches to growth. Each wave has its own nuances. Diets have cycled from a focus on protein to vegetables, back and forth. As the cycle repeats, attitudes are formed and reformed. Vegetarianism has moved from having its roots in animal cruelty and health to encompassing other global issues such as the carbon footprint of beef versus beets.

Equally interesting are trends that conflict. Two trends may be in full force but at the same time appear to be at odds. Take a look at the food versus fuel debate.

Corn has become the new fuel as improved methods of turning it into ethanol have met with government subsidies, taking significant amounts of corn out of the food chain. Add to this the use of corn in animal feed and in making new plastics, and you have a perfect storm of clashing trends. With world food concerns and costs increasing, tensions have arisen regarding the use of this key crop. The conflict is now accelerating the pursuit of non-food-based sources of fuel, such as grasses, which can also be used for ethanol.

At perhaps a more personal level, consider the clash between a desire to be connected 24/7 and a trend toward unplugging.

People no longer consider themselves to be online or offline, because with smart phones we are in a constant state of connectivity. At the same time there is a countertrend toward disconnecting. The result? Problems with sleep. On the one hand some people keep their phone in the bedroom, alerted all night of incoming messages, creating conflicts in relationships. Others are trying to disconnect by putting the phone to sleep in hopes of getting some themselves. Technology's role began with built-in settings to silence devices and dim screens at night. Now those same devices can monitor sleep cycles. They recommend lifestyle changes and feature gentler, natural-light alarm systems—creating even more incentives to tuck the phone under the pillow.

Divergent trends are not just external forces; they can be experienced as very personal dilemmas creating conflicts within ourselves and our most important relationships. When we step back and examine conflicting trends rather than taking bets on which will win out, we can look for ways to resolve the conflicts and discover new opportunity.

Divergence, not convergence, reveals unseen opportunities.

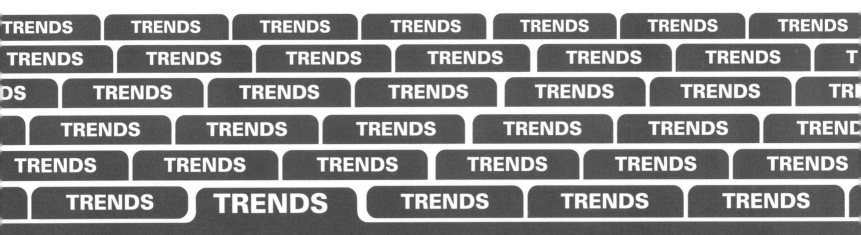

Impact trends

The problem with seeing opportunity in trends is that the amount of change one must absorb is overwhelming, often leaving us paralyzed. Even when we put a concerted effort into digesting all the change, it is daunting to figure out which shifts will be most relevant to us and how exactly they will impact us. After all, not all change will directly affect us, just as not all weather in the world will show up on our doorstep. What we need are impact trends—a downlisted set of trends that is relevant to our organization. Trends reports often come neatly packaged in predictable buckets, organized into catalogs of economic, ecological, social, demographic, and regulatory change. But these become much more interesting and actionable when we look at them through the eyes of the company and its opportunity drivers.

🌳 John Deere did this. Deere determined its growth essence—the key drivers of success. Deere is successful because the company pursues opportunities that are connected to the land, help customers get work done, and drive customer profitability. This is true across all their businesses, whether the opportunities are in agriculture, construction, forestry, consumer lawn and turf, or finance. So, rather than ask how the world is changing, we look at how the land is changing, how work is changing, and how customer profitability is changing. We pull trends across the Six Sources, mega and micro, seeds and cycles, and form a view of the future of land, work, and profit. Land changes alone span water shortages to urbanization, emissions regulations to shrinking yard sizes. Impact trends unite diverse forces around a common theme and provide greater direction toward what might be relevant in the future. 🌳

Like a group of meerkats scanning the horizon, our whole organization can be on the lookout!

Impact trends make sense to the organization. People at all levels can see why a set of trends about their business is important. This relevancy helps people in the organization to be trend watchers themselves.

It is better to have 10,000 people thinking about 10 trends than 10 people thinking about 10,000 trends.

> "The future creates the present. If you want to change what you are doing today, change your image of the future."
>
> *Glen Hiemstra, author and founder of Futurist.com*

View of the future

As we pull together impact trends we can form our unique view of the future. This is not a view of OUR future, but a view of THE future of the world that is relevant specifically to us. For Deere it was a view of the future of land, work, and customer profitability that guided them in identifying and selecting opportunities. Our view of the future depends not only on how broadly we look at trends but also on our time horizon. A food company may look out five years because this horizon is most meaningful to its brands and consumer preferences. An aerospace company may instead look out 20 years because of its development times. The farther out we look, the broader our Growth Horizon and the more opportunities we are likely to discover. If our view is three years we will see opportunities that will arise up to year three.

We will not see emerging trends that will affect us come year five but for which we need to prepare today.

The farther out we look, the more likely we are to see the forest for the trees.

We form our unique view of the future to plan our opportunity strategy. How often, though, have organizations planned their growth strategy by first looking at their capabilities rather than the future? It is a common philosophy that starts with where we are now and moves to where we could be next—a mind-set of growing from the core. **Looking to our capabilities rather than the future to guide growth is akin to the explorer looking to the rudders for direction rather than looking to the horizon.** By starting with our capabilities we won't see the changes in our environment that lead to adjacent opportunities. Many of today's careers didn't exist 20 years ago and it follows that in 20 years there will be a great many careers that we don't know of today. To plan our opportunity vision based on our capabilities today is quite myopic. It is the difference between looking out a window versus looking at a mirror. Both are looking at the glass—but one will show us what is possible while the other reflects who we are today. We risk missing the opportunities as they approach, or worse, not seeing a storm coming! Trends are our first Opportunity Finding tool and help form our horizon for growth.

Our growth potential is inextricably linked to our vision. What we see pretty much defines how far we travel and the direction we choose to travel in.

OPPORTUNITY THINKING

Change is an author of opportunity.

It comes in different sizes and volumes from a **SHOUT** to a whisper.

Change shuffles the deck, dealing us new cards and new opportunity.

Opportunity emerges when we embrace change rather than brace for it.

BIG
DIMENSIONS

Work Out: Opportunity Dimensions

⚓ Most have heard of Columbus—Christopher, that is. Less known is his brother Bartholomew who was a cartographer. If it wasn't for him the trip would never have been taken. It was his sketched maps of lands unseen that he and his brother used to pitch their plan to find a western route to the Indies. It was no easy task to kick-start the adventure. Bartholomew went off to persuade England's King Henry VII and France's Charles VIII while Christopher pitched the plan to Isabella I of Castile and Ferdinand II of Aragon. In the end, Bartholomew's maps were the key to convincing the crown to finally invest in the crazy scheme of discovery. ⚓

What map will persuade our organizations to journey to new lands?

Cartographers use latitude, longitude, and altitude to map lands and oceans. These dimensions helped explorers see where they were, where they could go, and where not to go. Our opportunity landscapes also have dimensions that help us pinpoint our current position and plot unknown areas. These Opportunity Dimensions are the basis for our opportunity cartography. They help us stretch to new places, see where our competitors are, and discover areas of unexplored opportunities.

> ❝For the wise man looks into space and he knows there are no limited dimensions.❞
>
> *Lao Tzu, philosopher of Taoism*

The dimensions of the opportunity landscape are our second Opportunity Finder. They start within each of the Six Sources. Business models range from bargain to premium, markets from young to old, resources from abundant to scarce, brands from big to small, technologies from high to low, and organizations from insourcing to outsourcing. Within each of the Sources there is a plethora of dimensions.

ELDERLY

OLD

ADULTS

TEENS

TWEENS

YOUNG

CHILDREN

Stretching dimensions

Let's look at life stages. Most companies and brands target a specific segment. Perhaps it is children, tweens, teens, adults, or the elderly. While we often look at markets through these segments, looking at them as a continuum can expand our view of opportunity.

🌱 A baby products company might stretch from infant into toddler products or perhaps stretch back and try to make their brand relevant earlier, during pregnancy or even conception.

A growing brand in the baby market came from a book. *What to Expect When You're Expecting* was published in 1986. It spurred a second book, *What to Expect in the First Year*. Since then the franchise has stretched to include books on other life stages including what to expect . . . before you

are expecting, in the 1st and 2nd years, for toddlers and preschool. They have expanded into a moment in time—*What to Expect at Bedtime*! The result is 13 books in the series, 34 million sold, in 30 languages, distributed across much of the world, and a variety of accessories such as charts and planners. They have expanded into the new medium of a movie with an all-star cast, and a new business structure—a nonprofit foundation in partnership with the Bill and Melinda Gates Foundation and the U.S. State Department. It is dedicated to prenatal health for impoverished women. The franchise has navigated along the life stage dimension uncovering new growth opportunities along the way. 🌱

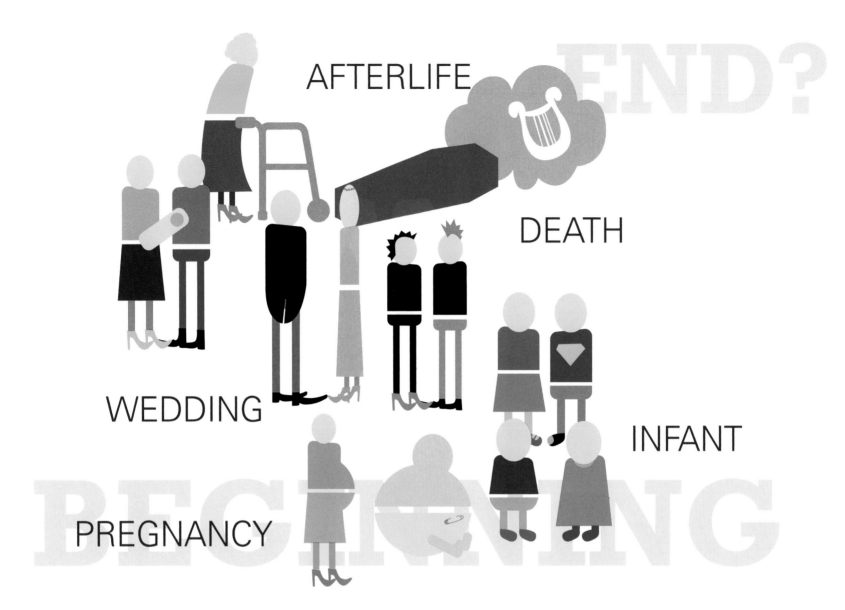

AFTERLIFE

END?

DEATH

WEDDING

INFANT

PREGNANCY

BEGINNING

🌱 Let's look at another category across the life stage. Social media started on college campuses but didn't stay there. They quickly expanded as they found opportunity by stretching to teens and subsequently growing by targeting older audiences as well as preteens and children. Stretching even further, they are now exploring how digital property is handled after death. A loved one's online profile on Facebook can become a place to post and share remembrances.🌱

Companies find further opportunity by magnifying a single point on a dimension.

🌱 Consider the humble flip-flop sandals—a favorite of children to adults. It would seem they have penetrated almost every life stage. But in the middle there was more room for growth. A brief but important moment in life—the wedding! Flip-flops, albeit satin ones, are now worn by blushing brides and their bridesmaids in both informal and very formal weddings.🌱

Business models may similarly be dimensionalized. Perhaps the most common dimension is low price to high price.

🌱 The bottled water category would typically fall at the lower end of the continuum with price ranges of 25 cents to a few dollars. Hotels have stretched this dimension by charging a premium for an in-room bottle ranging from $3 to about $20. Alternatively, some organizations buy in bulk and give them away as promotional items. But if you go to the other extreme there is new opportunity. Hawaii Deep Marine is extracting water from a depth of 915 feet and selling 2 ounce bottles for $33.50. Bling H_2O, developed by a Hollywood producer, is encrusted with Swarovski crystals from Austria and sells for up to $75 a bottle. It doesn't stop there though. Designer Altamirano created a 24 carat gold-coated bottle that is a tribute to Italian artist Modigliani. It contains water gathered from France, Fiji, and a glacier in Finland, along with a bit of gold dust . . . in the water! It was auctioned for $60,000 with proceeds going to the Planet Foundation to combat global warming. Still not smacking of ultraluxury? Perhaps a bottle of Aurum will do. You can find it at the Big Boys Toys luxury exhibition in the Middle East. Made of crystal, covered in 24 carat gold, with 113 diamonds, it contains water from St. Leonhard in Germany and, of course, drinkable gold flake. Price tag? $900,000.

What might be beyond these end points? Paying people to drink water? Don't be surprised! Some health programs are incentivizing people to take actions to live healthy. Almost anything is possible when you stretch thinking to new dimensions. 🌱

Converging discrete categories

Not all descriptions of opportunity would seem at first glance to lend themselves to being dimensionalized.

The product categories of food and beverage typically are treated as two separate categories. They reside in different parts of the store, have different packaging, and use different manufacturing processes. What happens when we take these discrete categories and explore them as a continuum? We find a continuum of converging forms of nutrition and opportunity.

FOODBEVERAGE

There has been significant growth in the number of calories consumed in liquid form. At the same time beverages have become more foodlike. Milk shakes have made way for smoothies. Athletes and active people who consume protein shakes are now exploring gels and slurries as supplements. The juicing industry—where food is turned into beverage—has boomed with new products, equipment, shops, and shows. Food-derived milks are on the rise, starting with soy and rice milk and now moving toward almond and oat milks. While oat-based beverages are popular in Central and South America, they are new to many. The Naked brand is now building on the convergence trend by combining oat milks with fruit to create new and delicious smoothies. What's beyond liquid food? Some creative spirits are investigating inhaled nutrition, with aerosol powder sprays such as Aeroshot's caffeine energy product.

Success comes from breaking and reinventing convention.

> " Our mind is capable of passing beyond the line we have drawn for it. Beyond the pairs of opposites of which the world consists, other insights begin. "

Herman Hesse, German-Swiss author and artist

Exploring opposites

Finding apparent opposite ends of a dimension also allows us to explore ways to remove the distance between them, looping endpoints back together. Consider merging the opposites of free and premium.

🌱 Providing software products for free then charging for complementary products or advanced features is a business model called freemium. Services such as Skype's VoIP Internet calling, Evernote's personal data collection, and LinkedIn's professional networking are based on the freemium model. Driven by the low cost of production and the networking effects of the Internet, this business model depends on converting a portion of free users to purchasers of paid services or products while those using the free products provide value by spreading the word and providing feedback. 🌱

Challenging assumptions

Dimensionalizing opportunity helps us expand our vision beyond its normal ranges and limits, going outside our preconceptions to enter a new realm of possibilities. To do this we must continually unfold the dimensions of what we know and stretch established frameworks. One of the most fixed sets of assumptions in business today revolves around brands. Companies often invest for years to build their brands only to find that they then struggle to see opportunity beyond or between their brands. Soon their brands are working hard, but they are not getting the growth they deserve, mired in incremental innovation at best or cannibalizing extensions at worst. While the guardrails of brand equity are very important in the final implementation of an idea, they should not be step one in the opportunity-finding process.

Looking at brands through the eyes of opportunity rather than looking at the opportunity through the eyes of the brand will open up new ways to extend and even develop new brands. This is the fundamental difference between brand growth and stretch. A brand growth approach starts by exploring opportunity and then maps brands onto them, allowing us to look at areas thought of as outside the brand, between brands, or even offbrand. This opens up greater potential for growth from hitherto unseen opportunities. Alternatively, brand stretch starts with the brand and uses its narrow lens to look at opportunity. It is inherently limited in its growth potential.

Brands are dimensions, not centers of inescapable gravitational pull.

Brand growth

❦ Japanese Yamaha and UK-based Virgin Group are two brands that are anything but a black hole of gravitational pull. They have both taken brand growth, rather than brand stretch, approaches. They have looked for opportunity and then used brand strength to capture them. Yamaha started in musical instruments in 1887 and has since gone into motorcycles, sporting goods, semiconductors, and digital sound production including sound generators for mobile phones.

Virgin was started by Sir Richard Branson as a record store in the 1970s. The Virgin brand has now been extended to over 400 companies including airlines, hotels, trains, radio, cosmetics, mortgages, wine, energy, mobile phones, hot air balloons, deep sea submarines, and space tourism to name a few. There have been flops, such as when Virgin tried to take on Coca-Cola and Pepsi with Virgin cola or when they created a rival to iTunes. But the successes have far outweighed the failures.

Both Yamaha and Virgin have had the boldness to take the strength of their name and reputation and move into wildly adjacent areas. ❦

Opportunity dimensions offer endless ways to stretch, magnify, connect, or upend our understanding of where there is potential for growth. We use them to map the contours of the opportunity landscape. Like any map, we can use the dimensions to look at our landscape at a 50,000-foot view down to a microscopic view. They provide a framework for easily moving from one view to another.

We build maps through collections of opportunity dimensions across the landscape—resembling the lines of latitude or the contours on a topographical map. These form the backbone of our opportunity cartography. The resulting maps help us visualize what might be only conceptualized. So often in our organizations discussions about opportunities go around and around because people can't see where opportunity is and where it is not. This is understandable because new opportunities are typically in unfamiliar territory. Opportunity cartography reduces the sense of unfamiliarity and uncertainty. The maps create a healthy curiosity about the areas likely to contain riches, all the while reassuring us that those areas are not outside the realm of possibility.

A picture is worth a thousand words. If you want to convince people to go somewhere, a map just might be the most compelling way to launch a new voyage.

> "The contour of the land is an aid to an army . . . Those who do battle knowing these will win, those who do battle without knowing these will lose."

Sun Tzu, author The Art of War

Opportunities are spatial in nature.

Dimensions help us stretch opportunity and ourselves.

The more space we see and understand, the more opportunity we find.

Dimensions free us from the gravitational pull of our current positions.

BIG INSIGHTS

Find Out: Opportunity Insights

 Someone had to stock the ship for Columbus's voyages, and the task fell to Amerigo Vespucci. His curiosity got the better of him, though, and he soon joined at least two expeditions himself. Upon his return from one journey he wrote to his sponsor, Lorenzo de' Medici, and detailed the flora and fauna, currents of the Amazon, and the star movements that he observed. He concluded that the land could not be the Asian continent Columbus supposed it to be. It had to be an entirely new continent with its own characteristics. His letters detailing the land and people, including tantalizing details of their practices in marriage and childbirth were so interesting they were translated into multiple languages and widely published, becoming even more popular than Columbus's accounts!

Insights are our third Opportunity Finder. The notion of insight as a tool to understand opportunity is not a new one. Insights in one shape or form have been steering the success of individuals and organizations for a very long time. From Archimedes' "Eureka!" moment of enlightenment to methodical research, rich insights have been the catalysts of growth. Throughout history, having a deep understanding of something has been the underpinning of both the intuitive hunch and the calculated decision.

Market research has been the backbone of our insight gathering. It typically consists of asking questions of our customers and consumers, both current and potential, and gleaning value from their answers. Yet, getting the right answers assumes we are asking the right questions of the right people. Given the surprising failures of products from companies with significant investment in their market research functions, we might wonder if we aren't missing something. Perhaps gathering insights for opportunity exploration requires something more. **So how are opportunity insights more than just market insights?**

Our consumers do not hold a monopoly on insight.

Consumers are influenced by others around them who may not directly have any stake in our brands or products. These influencers span the kaleidoscope of communities across the opportunity ecosystem. They often know and can describe attitudes and behaviors better than consumers themselves.

" Where the telescope ends, the microscope begins. Which of the two has the grander view? "

Victor Hugo, poet, author

Applying an opportunity lens to discovery means that people across all Six parts of the ecosystem can provide us with insights on where growth will come from. Opinion leaders such as technologists, financial analysts, brand owners, designers, the media, bloggers, and activists live in the opportunity ecosystem and can bring us observations and projections because they know its nuances far better than we do. They have insight for today and the future because they not only observe the opportunities, they influence what's hot and what's not. They open our eyes to new needs and wants, inform us of new technologies and ways to create value, or apprise us of the conditions favorable or unfavorable to our interests. Whether they are influencers or just observers, they have fresh eyes and ears.

Consider the challenge of trying to get new insights on the snack preferences of children at school.

Executives at the Kellogg's cereal and snack company felt they had learned all they could about school snacks from their market research with mothers and children. The question was—how could they get a new perspective? The answer was in the ecosystem. It wasn't from opinion leaders though; it was from janitors in the school lunchrooms. They knew everything that was eaten, thrown away, thrown in food fights, and traded on the cafeteria black market.

Opportunity insights go beyond product and market insights. Tapping into the ecosystem provides us with insights into organizational processes, manufacturing, relationships in the environment, and business model.

Consider the innovations in America's pastime—baseball. In 2002 a man named Billy Bean listened to the new age statistics of innovators such as Bill James. SaberMetrics brought Bean, the general manager for the Oakland A's, a new way of identifying undervalued players. It was a statistical model he had built that would calculate a player's potential rather than use the traditional, seasoned eyes and ears of the scouts. The model was truly disruptive. It upended how teams chose players, and it gave the A's—a team with a low budget—an amazing run to the playoffs. It met with a lot of resistance—seen as turning a beloved sport into moneyball. But as the A's, with their relatively miniscule budget, stacked up the wins, other teams began to pay attention. Eventually the other teams adopted the model or, in the case of the Boston Red Sox, hired James and developed their own.

The story doesn't end there. Billy Bean continues his openness to the ecosystem and is now developing a new model, a model that adds back the views of the scouts and new indicators of the psychological make-up of a player. Do they have the mental and emotional mettle to withstand the show—the pressures of Major League ball? He is gathering all the insights, using all the tools at his disposal to create a model of prediction.

We, too, should use every insight possible to expand our thinking.

R+D
IN
PROGRESS

CAUTION

R+D
IN
PROGRESS

Tapping into the internal ecosystem

It's not just the external ecosystem that is a valuable source of insight. Let's look to our own organizations for fresh perspectives. Each part of our organization will have a different view of the world, having brushed up against opportunity throughout their travels. Technologists will see the cutting edge where innovative advances can drive opportunity. Manufacturing will see opportunity in cost reductions. Business leaders will see bounty in attractive acquisitions. We often struggle with insight gathering internally even more than externally. But the same methods that work to gain customer insights can be used to pull insights from our own staff.

Our colleagues can go one step further beyond providing us with their own insights; they can also join us in becoming the researchers themselves. Most people have relationships across the external ecosystem and can tap into those relationships to gain new perspectives. People across the functions can join with the market research teams to listen to customers and consumers and, in doing so, the extra ears in the room will hear new things. Technologists and designers hear ways to solve problems that might get lost in translation. Brand owners catch whiffs of new positionings. Manufacturing understands requirements first hand.

If you want to make it even richer, get more senior people involved. It may have been a while since leaders have brushed shoulders with a real, live consumer. Leaders will pick up new insights because they are responsible for a broader array of business elements and can sometimes connect dots others don't. Often there are simply too many layers between those who gather the insights and those who define and choose the opportunities, letting rich discoveries slip through our fingers during the distilling process.

Organizations know less than the sum of the knowledge of the employees.

Ecosystem as researchers

Bringing an opportunity lens to insights means we broaden both who we talk to and who does the listening thus drawing in both the external and internal ecosystems. Doing this is but half the battle, though. People can only tell us so much. They often struggle to tell us things they want because they can't fully imagine anything different from what they have today. These are the needs and wants unleashed by great invention. Opportunity insights require that we go beyond what people can tell us to learn what hasn't been articulated.

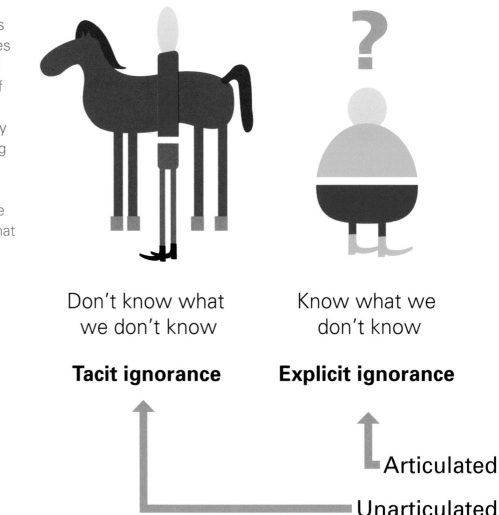

Don't know what we don't know

Tacit ignorance

Know what we don't know

Explicit ignorance

Articulated

Unarticulated

66 If I had asked people what they wanted, they would have said faster horses. 99

Henry Ford, inventor, manufacturer

Opportunity insights are more than knowledge.

They are knowledge with a life.

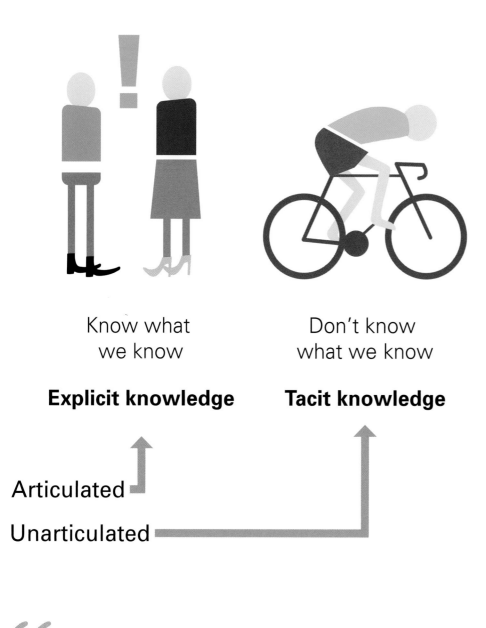

Know what
we know

Explicit knowledge

Don't know
what we know

Tacit knowledge

Articulated

Unarticulated

66... above all watch with glittering
eyes the whole world around you
because the greatest secrets are
hidden in the most unlikely places.99

Roald Dahl, author of Charlie and the Chocolate Factory

Articulating the unarticulated

Insights are not all created equal. There is a continuum of attitudes, behaviors, needs, and wishes that we can and cannot articulate. We start exploring opportunities by simply learning what we already know— surfacing the treasure troves of insights from our own organizations. In doing so it is inevitable that we will start to make a wish list of things we would like to know. Now we know what we don't know. Articulating what we know and what we don't know is the relatively easy part.

Another realm of insight lies in the unarticulated. There are some things people know, but can't bring to the surface: habits that cannot be described, cunning processes long forgotten, skills we can't quite teach. Like riding a bike, we don't know how to articulate some of the things we know. Our knowledge has become tacit, escaping the fingers of language and cloaking opportunities to be found in entrenched work-arounds and long-ago accepted inefficiencies. This applies both to our company and to the world at large. Throughout the ecosystem, people struggle to put their finger on it, to state the obvious. But the obvious may be precisely where innovation is most needed. It often is only through observation that we unlock these insights.

Ask us what we need in the way of a carrot, and few of us would have much to say. Carrots are the first thing to go on party trays. They are popular when someone else has gone to the trouble of peeling, slicing, and chopping them. Did you ever notice, though, that people aren't fond of carrots when they have been quartered and the core begins to dry. These observations led to the advent of the baby carrot. Baby carrots aren't really baby carrots, by the way. They are mechanically peeled and shaved down to create a tapered miniature where the core is protected to maintain moisture for long-term snacking. While this specific product was a big (albeit miniature) success, the insight shed light on a wider opportunity for ready-to-eat fruit and veggies in general, from snack bags of snow peas to apple slices packaged with caramel, prechopped broccoli and cauliflower to mini lunch trays resplendent with paired veggies, cheeses, and dips.

Equally elusive is when we don't know what we don't know—when we can't describe what would be ideal because we haven't the technologists' and designers' brilliance in creating new-to-the-world value.

> "Discovery consists of seeing what everybody has seen and thinking what nobody has thought."
>
> *Albert von Szent-Györgyi, Nobel Prize winner, discovered vitamin C*

Who would have thought there was any opportunity in kitchen utensils, those long-evolved mainstays of cooking? But one man observed his wife's painful attempts to work with current utensils to accommodate her arthritis. He pinpointed an unmet need and used it to design a more delightful and ergonomically friendly can opener. It gently separates and pulls the lid off rather than cutting metal and features large handles for better grip and less strain. A series of similarly fashioned, ergonomically smart, and distinctly styled black handled utensils followed. Widely popular, consumers bought new kitchen utensils, replacing ones they had been perfectly satisfied with and never found wanting. The OXO Company grew out of a single observation. Determined that kitchen tools should not hurt, Sam Farber perfected ergonomic designs of 15 tools. OXO found ready demand with $3 million in revenue in the first year, an average sales growth of 27% per year over the company history, and numerous design awards. The OXO story is one of capturing an opportunity that existed all along but had gone unnoticed.

Language restricts innovation to what can be described; visualization breaks boundaries.

Articulating the unarticulated is both art and science. It can come by finding ecosystem members who can articulate what consumers cannot, or by finding and observing unusual users or unusual uses of products. Sometimes it comes from examining compensating behaviors that people use to get around a problem. It could be discovered by carefully mining dissatisfaction or fractures in brand loyalty. We can help people articulate more by using design to prod these insights free. Just as an inkblot test unearths the psyche, so design can be used to spur new insight.

Use design as a research stimulus, not just a research outcome!

Opportunity insight goes beyond the who and what of opportunity to the where, how, when, and why. This means it will be an effort that likely requires both observation and conversation, stimulation and experimentation, and it will be helped immensely by engaging the internal and external ecosystem both as the study participant and researcher. Tapping into the ecosystem rather than just the consumer solves a challenge that market researchers have long been faced with, namely that they are often constrained to asking about preferences within a time frame the consumer is able to predict, which isn't very long. But R+D organizations need insights further out in order to pursue technologies that take longer to develop. Because opportunities are both near and far, using an opportunity lens encourages us to seek ecosystem experts who think further into the future.

> "Skeptical scrutiny is the means by which deep insights can be winnowed from deep nonsense."
>
> *Carl Sagan, astrophysicist, author*

Opportunity insights come from the ecosystem, not just the market.

Six Sources of insight enrich a view of opportunity.

The ecosystem and design can lead to articulating the unarticulated.

BIG
PICTURE

Maps are the most enduring evidence of explorations.

Imagine coming across a document written over 1,000 years ago, translating it, and sparking hundreds of years of discovery as a result! In 1400 Emanual Chrysoloras, a Byzantine scholar, dusted off Ptolemy's *Geography*, which was written in 150 AD. Ptolemy had mapped the world as it was known—all the way from the Canary Islands to the coast of Cambodia, charting over 4,500 cities! He even used a grid system that was a predecessor to latitude and longitude.

Chrysoloras translated it into Latin making it more accessible, and then later it was printed and widely distributed. The field of cartography was reborn!

Soon all kinds of maps were created and in all kinds of forms. Some had north at the top and others had south at the top. Some showed only land and water while others annotated the land with information on plants, animals, and historical events. In 1492 Martin Behaim created the Erdapfel—or Earth Apple—better known as the first globe. In 1548 Giacomo Gastaldi created the first pocket size atlas. Maps varied based on the needs of the user and the information being conveyed. But the advent of these maps and their distribution were credited with emboldening hundreds to venture out on new expeditions.

Cartography today also produces a wide variety of maps: topographical and roadmaps, maps of resources, political maps, weather maps, and maps that show physical or thematic features. While the styles and content vary, the goal of cartography is always the same—model reality so it can be communicated, reducing complexity to that which is needed for the intended audience.

Exploring opportunities calls for equally creative ways of representing information. **Our organizations deserve better representations of our discoveries if we expect them to launch out on a journey with us.**

Opportunity cartography

Bringing together our three opportunity finders of trends, dimensions, and insights gives us what we need to build an overall picture of opportunity. These maps can provide significant value for our organizations.

It is hard to appreciate just how valuable maps of newly explored territories were during the Age of Exploration given the proliferation of maps we have today. They were so valuable that a black market arose where maps were sold to competing countries. Maps of opportunities are no less valuable today as they too provide real competitive advantage. **Yet few organizations do more than create endless documents and spreadsheets, none of which really paint a picture of where to go.** We can build real, visual maps that define our Opportunity Landscape.

Like the field of cartography, Opportunity cartography also results in a wide range of styles of maps whose visualization may vary from company to company and landscape to landscape. The goal of mapping is always the same though, to show relationship between the components of the landscape. Each opportunity finder brings a different view, but at the same time they inform each other. Key trends suggest novel dimensions we can use to define a space differently. The dimensions form the structure of the landscape onto which we layer the trends and new insights. Insights stretch the dimensions and reveal white spaces. We combine all three onto a single map, and the opportunity landscape really comes to life.

> ❝The soul never thinks without a picture.❞
>
> *Aristotle, philosopher*

To illustrate we can look at the trends, dimensions, and insights in a simple snacking example. Consider two trends: weight concerns and snacking. These two trends are inherently at odds yet both are on the rise.

For years food manufacturers innovated on calorie reduction by developing low-fat replacements and artificial sweeteners.

UNDERWEIGHT

LOW CALORIE

100cals

Number of meals per day is on the rise

Snacking is replacing full meals

HIGH CALORIE

SNACKING IS ON THE INCREASE

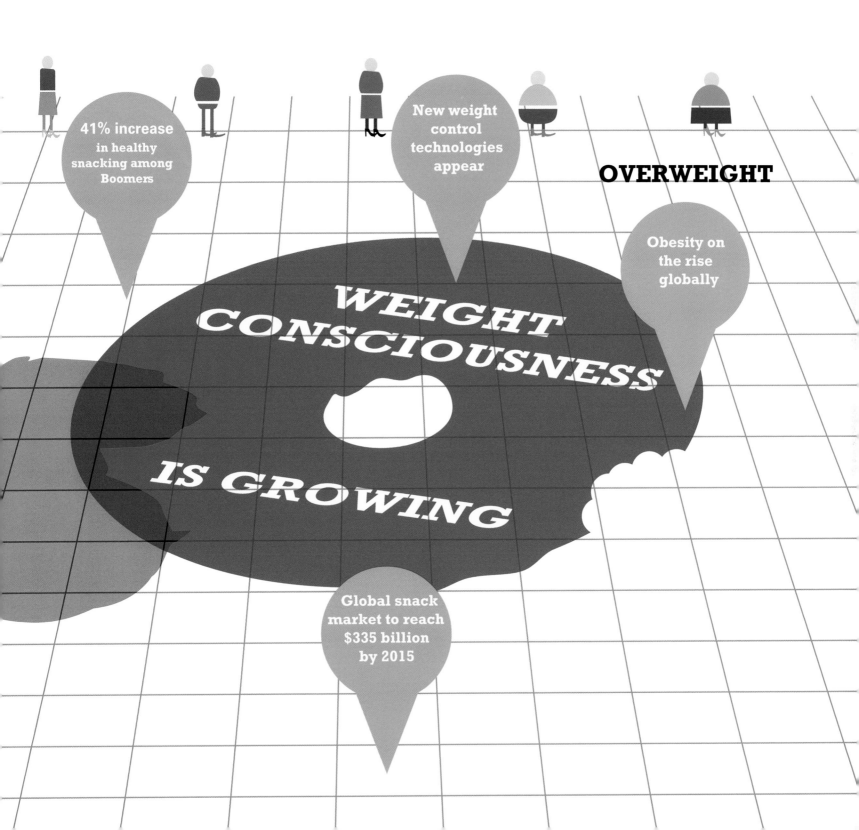

Low calorie foods—regular calorie foods

Insights revealed that people were loyal to the taste of their full-calorie favorites, and the lighter-calorie options simply didn't taste as good. Recognizing this led to diets that allowed for the occasional splurge with a favorite treat but in small quantities. Unfortunately, keeping the quantities small turned out to be a big struggle for most people. Portion control was a real challenge.

Nabisco observed the challenge and saw opportunity. They switched attention from creating diet foods to creating diet packs. What could be easier for the consumer than grabbing a portion-controlled pack, only 100 calories, guaranteed? Packaging, rather than tweaking the food, allowed the weight-conscious to return to their favorite foods with a little extra help in self-control. This benefit turned a profit: snack packs averaged 20% more profitability than larger packages. Nabisco started the craze and within just a year Kellogg's and General Mills followed.

Portions: consumer-controlled to company-controlled

As with all opportunity, change is the only constant. The landscape changed, and Nabisco came under fire for promoting consumption of empty calories, so they discontinued their 100-calorie pack line. The opportunity they discovered was still there though. Other snack food companies adopted the 100-calorie number as a signal of healthy indulgence and combined it with additional nutritional claims around fiber, protein, and satisfaction. From Emerald nut mixes to Ocean Spray's craisins, Orville Redenbacher popcorn, and several brands of protein bars, the new snack packs were a welcome addition to the dieter's cupboard. Nabisco reintroduced the packs due to popular demand and enhanced the offer with thinner formulations. Opportunity was the result of a confluence of trends, insights, and new dimensions.

The choices of opportunity direction are the luxury of those who already have opportunities from which to choose. Discovering opportunities is really our greatest challenge. But big opportunities don't hang out on street corners wearing "I'm a BIG opportunity" T-shirts. If they were that obvious they would have been capitalized on long ago and would no longer be much of an opportunity.

They require some hard work to track down and map out.

> **Opportunity is missed by most people because it is dressed in overalls and looks like work.**
>
> *Thomas Edison, inventor*

Some people will see opportunity everywhere. They will focus on the outcomes of all opportunities and therefore see opportunities as rabbits that should all be chased down. Some will struggle to see any opportunity. They will favor the lowest risk ventures. Others will no doubt focus on their areas of expertise, preferring options with little to no uncertainty.

The opportunities we see are too often a function of our intuition, our functional lens, and our predisposition to see the glass as half full or half empty.

Regardless of our disposition, we have no guarantee that the obvious opportunities will be very big or even truly be born of a confluence of need, an ability to create value, and the right conditions. We need a more reliable view of what is possible. Opportunity cartography, mapping our opportunity landscape, provides us with that view.

OPPORTUNITY THINKING

***Opportunity cartography paints
a picture of our opportunity landscape.***

It brings together all three opportunity
finders into a cohesive story.

Visualizing opportunity gives us a map
with which to launch a journey.

CHAPTER 5

BIG
LANDSCAPE

🚢 A German cartographer, a proofreader, a Latinist, and the nephew of a saint all got together one day to do a puzzle. They met high in the mountains of what is now Alsace Lorraine, France, in 1507. The puzzle they were trying to complete was the map of the world. The pieces were comprised of accounts of journeys and pictures of bits of the world. Some of the pieces were Ptolemy's; some were the accounts of Bartholomew Columbus and Amerigo Vespucci; and some were scattered pages bought on the black market. There may even have been pieces from Chinese explorations as there is speculation that perhaps this is how the mapmakers gained insights regarding the Rocky Mountains of North America and the Andes of South America—both of which had not yet been explored by Europeans.

When the puzzle was finished, a new picture emerged. A picture of the world as having four major parts rather than three. Common belief had been that there was only Europe, Asia, and Africa. The thinking was so deeply ingrained that when Columbus brought to light an entirely new land, it was not recognized as such for years. It wasn't until this team of scholars started putting the puzzle pieces together, reading the writings of the explorers, and studying the travelogues that they saw the world for more of what it was. 🚢

Exploring and mapping new lands is not enough. We need to interpret what we have found, and structure how we will think about the opportunities. Framing how we view opportunities is critical for decisions about effort and investment. Accurately describing the landscape, the territories, and the regions within is critical for us staying focused on what is in and what is out from a strategic standpoint. Understanding the borders correctly and being able to communicate them to our organization, understanding the shape of the shorelines, and accurately showing where opportunity lies, aids deciding what and how we will pursue it.

Mapping the opportunity landscape is a lot like doing a puzzle. Most of us have put together a puzzle or two in our lifetime. We start by deciding just how ambitious we want to be: 2,000; 1,000; 500; or 100 pieces? We also pick the puzzle by the picture on the box cover—a landscape or image we are drawn to. Next we open the box to an unwieldy jumble of pieces and start making sense of the mess. But where do we start? With the edge pieces, of course!

We begin by defining the borders.

The pieces of our opportunity landscape are the opportunity finders: the trends, dimensions, and insights across the Six Sources. The size of our opportunity landscape is like the size of a puzzle. We can pick a big or small landscape to pursue. The edge pieces are the key dimensions that help create the boundaries or edges of our exploration.

Companies describe their opportunity landscape in different ways. A global food company might see it broadly as nutrition with enjoyment, while a smaller food company might define it strictly as baked snacks. The scope, like the size of the puzzle, will depend on how much the company can take on. The definition of the landscape could stay the same for years and then begin to shift as the markets they serve shift. Sometimes a company will even make dramatic changes to its definition of their landscape.

Our definition of our landscape will dramatically affect how our stakeholders, stockholders, and ecosystem see us. It is the beginning of our growth vision because it tells where we plan to grow.

DuPont began as an explosives company in 1802 and moved to chemicals and materials in its second century. Now the company is building capabilities in the biological and life sciences. These shifts may appear dramatic, but look deeper and we can see the starting points of new opportunity. DuPont chose to build on its scientific and materials capabilities by establishing a major scientific center, the DuPont Experimental Station, in 1903. That enabled the company to move into polymer research and development in the 1920s and 1930s and grow the materials portfolio from there. As the materials sciences evolved it became clear by the 1980s that adding biological sciences to chemistry, materials, and engineering would position the company for new opportunities in the 21st century.

DuPont followed through with a series of acquisitions that led to new thinking and capabilities in agriculture, food, and biotechnology. DuPont acquired Pioneer, a seed company, in 1999. They entered into a joint venture with Bunge in 2003 for healthy soy ingredients which led to the full ownership of Solae in 2012. The shift toward biology was further crystallized with the acquisition, in 2012, of Danisco, which had both food businesses and the biotech company Genencor. Expanding bioscience also meant divesting less related units such as legacy textile fibers businesses, and automotive and industrial coatings. This further consolidated DuPont's shift from a chemical and materials company to a science company with businesses in agriculture, biotechnology, and materials sciences.

OPPORTUNITY THINKING

A landscape of opportunity awaits us.

How we define our landscape both inspires and bounds our growth vision.

Our landscapes may stay the same for years and then change as opportunity moves.

BIG
SPACES

Let's go back to the mountains for a moment. Besides putting together the puzzle pieces into a cohesive picture, our team of scholars had to come up with names for the new places. What do you name a continent? They settled on the name America, named after Amerigo Vespucci, who they saw as instrumental in discovering the land's true identity. The Spanish weren't too thrilled. They felt the land should have been named after Columbus. But with 1,000 of the team's brand new atlases in print, the name stuck.

Explorers and cartographers wielded lasting power as they defined and named the territories within the lands they reached. Cabot explored the northern reaches defining the area known as Newfoundland, named because it was a new-found-land. Ponce de León named La Florida "flowery land." Soon large territories were delineated—New France, New England, and Hispaniola—regions were defined and claims staked. Over time, through wars and treaties, negotiations and bartering, territories were redrawn, claimed, and named again. ⚓

Naming new places makes the discoveries about them stick. It creates excitement, curiosity, and vision of the new places. Cartographers played a big role in helping communicate the unknown, shaping how people thought, and crystalizing an understanding of what was known.

It's the same way in opportunity landscaping. Defining and naming the landscape makes it more understandable, more real, and a lot more inspiring. People know where they are going even if the places are unfamiliar to them. They are motivated by the aura of the name and can rally behind the grand vision of how to get there.

Naming an opportunity makes it concrete and aspirational. U.S. President John F. Kennedy did this when he said he wanted to put a man on the moon and return him safely before the decade was out. He could have waxed eloquent about NASA being a leader in space exploration, but instead he created an inspiring vision by naming and claiming where he wanted to go. Naming our opportunities is critical for achieving our goals.

Opportunity territories

Once our landscape has been identified and named, defining the opportunity territories is the next step for us. We move from a focus on the landscape to the areas within the landscape we want to pursue. Using the opportunity finders, we piece together areas that have a similar center of gravity, a similar cohesive nature that we can go after. So how do we do this?

Let's get back to our puzzle. We have the edges done—so now what? We separate the pieces into colors and subjects. Piles of reds, blues, and greens or sky, water, buildings, and ships begin to take form. We might divide and conquer—"you take the sailboats, and I'll work on the houses by the bay." In a similar way, the opportunity maker sorts through the opportunity finders to group them into territories of potential. Just as puzzle pieces are often grouped along different characteristics, so, too, the opportunity maker may define one territory by market, another around technology, and another around a new business model—recognizing that opportunity can spring from many Sources.

These apples to oranges definitions of opportunity territories show how different the opportunity landscaping approach is from traditional industry landscaping processes. In fact, opportunity landscaping is as different from industry landscaping as doing a puzzle is from playing solitaire. In both cases we have a lot of individual pieces that must be put in their places. Puzzle-making is like opportunity landscaping. We creatively sort the pieces through intuition and discovery. Playing solitaire is like industry landscaping. The pieces, or cards, fit into predetermined categories—the suits of diamonds, hearts, clubs, and spades. In traditional industry landscaping the sectors have also been predefined, often following long-standing industrial codes that are slow to change. All the companies in an industry utilize the same structure—the same information, market segments, and market sizing—often buying the same reports from the same industry research companies. The resulting insights are valuable, even critical, but they do not provide any competitive advantage nor do they point to opportunities that aren't obvious to all.

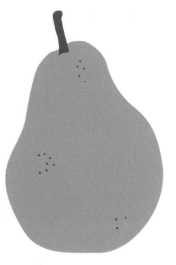

The mapmakers in the 1600s were not playing solitaire—they were putting together puzzles, because they were dealing with the unknown, the new. As lands and borders were better defined, structure began to emerge so that new discoveries about rivers, mountains, and resources could be put in their proper place—they could be anchored to something that was known. They were mapping new opportunities.

In opportunity landscaping we begin with little to no structure and must create structure intuitively. Over time the structure we create becomes useful for organizing our learning. But if we have done that landscaping properly, the structure will not look much like traditional industry landscaping. It will be unique to the opportunities available.

Opportunity landscaping is a creative, insight-driven, bottom-up process with which different organizations will arrive at different territories. In fact, two companies in the same industry should define their opportunities differently! The markets they operate in may be the same but their capabilities and ecosystem relationships will be different, meaning their opportunities will not be the same. Two food companies may operate in the same industry but will arrive at different opportunities. One may have deeper packaging and design capabilities, causing them to focus on premium and higher margin products, while the other may be stronger in their distribution causing them to focus on foods for convenience stores and food service. The capabilities determining the types of value they can create will vary, and their opportunities will take different shape.

Opportunity landscaping breaks down the imaginary walls built through industry landscaping. But it also breaks down the walls constructed within our own organizations. Corporations often define their opportunities along business unit lines, stating that opportunity resides in one business and not in another—creating organizational haves and have-nots! The winners get all the resources, and the losers are in a support role, which means that the organization has effectively disengaged half its workforce in pursuing new spaces. But it need not be so. It is much more powerful to define opportunities that cut across all the businesses, leveraging a broad range of talents, capabilities, minds, and hearts.

🌱 This is exactly how John Deere identified opportunities that cut across their businesses of agriculture, forestry, construction, wind power, commercial landscaping, and consumer products. Driving from their view of the future of land and work, and mapping this future against their abilities to create value, they arrived at several opportunity territories including worksite integration, machine productivity, and water. These territories deeply resonated across the businesses. They allowed for new corporate technology investments, new platforms that transcended organizational lines, and the potential to create entirely new businesses. The territories were so robust and powerful that they are still in effect after seven years and have been approached through innovation close to and far from the core. The opportunities for innovation stayed the same because they were locked into the essence of who Deere and Company is and locked into their view of the future. 🌱

" A genuine leader is not a searcher for consensus but a molder of consensus. "

Martin Luther King Jr., leader in the African-American civil rights movement

Opportunity spaces

⚓ Exploration didn't stop once the territories were defined. Traversing up and down coasts and rivers and mapping them helped explorers understand more of the terrain. But it did something else. It got to the heart of exploration—the good stuff—the reward. The explorers started to link up both the where and the what: Asia and silk, the East and spices, New England and wood, South America and cocoa, and regrettably, all too many areas were known for their slaves. ⚓

Once we have named the landscape and territories, we, too, explore what the territories have to offer. Each territory may initially be linked with a big win, such as silk, spices, or timber. But as we look more closely at the opportunity finders that sit within the territory—the trends, dimensions, and insights that pertain to a specific territory—we will see interesting opportunity spaces.

We have all done the same thing when we do a puzzle. The pieces in our piles—the blues, the greens, buildings, or sailboats—at first look all too similar, causing us to wonder how we will ever put them together. As we dive in, variations and subtleties come to light. We see different shades of blue in the sea, different textures in the trees and plants, and details we hadn't noticed before in the buildings and boats. We begin to form piles within piles creating groupings that have a higher probability of fitting together.

Similarly, once our opportunity territories take shape we identify spaces we can actually innovate against. These spaces are specific enough to allow development of product and service ranges.

🌳 For example, across the board food companies are determining how they will go after the territory of health and wellness. Vegetable company Del Monte might be keen to leverage the insights of Dr. Oz, one of the leading voices in health, who has recently touted canned and frozen vegetables as the affordable approach to healthy eating. Hormel, maker of the iconic Spam, might focus on increasing protein in diets, leveraging their healthy turkey brand Jennie-O. New Zealand-based dairy giant, Fonterra, may focus on finding ways to bring milk into new snacking occasions, as exemplified by their highly successful launch of Mammoth—a protein fortified coffee drink for men on the go. Alternatively, Whitewave, makers of Silk soy, rice, and almond milks, as well as organic dairy products, may focus on the origins of the food. One company will see opportunity around allergen-free foods; another will see it around local sourcing of ingredients to create a new brand proposition focused on the provenance or origin of the ingredients. The spaces look like apples to oranges with one space derived from a consumer trend and another derived from the technology, one from brand and another from supply chain. The ways a company defines these will be truly unique to them as a function of what they can bring to the table! 🌳

How companies define their territories and spaces is both a function of strategy and drives strategy. John Deere looked for territories that cut across their traditional lines of business, seeking corporate platforms for growth. Alternatively, Kraft foods saw such starkly different territories for growth in food they split into two companies! They were so convinced of the apples to oranges nature—the strategies that would cause them to win—they decided it was better to pursue those opportunities as entirely separate entities.

One territory was for opportunities in their North American grocery brands of Velveeta, Kraft Macaroni & Cheese, Jello, Planters nuts, and Oscar Mayer meats. These brands will see slow growth but good profits and lots of cash in the years to come. But don't associate slow growing with dull. Kraft is targeting three opportunity spaces that cut across these brands. More exciting flavors: onion, bacon, or tomato dipping sauces for Miracle Whip, jalapeño-flavored Philadelphia cream cheese, and cracked black pepper in Kraft string cheese; Convenience, with new prepared foods such as pulled pork from Oscar Mayer and Velveeta skillet dinners such as Jambalaya; and Customization, including expansion of their MiO brand energy drops, Crystal Light flavors for water, and A1 rubs and sauces.

The other territory being pursued by the new company, Mondelez, formed in 2012, is the faster growing international snacks category with brands including Oreo, recently acquired Cadbury, and Ritz. One opportunity space is chocolate, with Mondelez following a vision to be the world's largest chocolatier leveraging brands including Cadbury Dairy Milk, Milka, Toblerone, and Lacta. Spaces within spaces include three regions: India, Brazil, and Russia, and two innovation platforms: bubbly and bite-size chocolate. The company is looking at spaces at the intersection of brands, using Cadbury packaging style for Oreos in India and creating a Cadbury Milka Philadelphia cream cheese for Europe. Mondelez sees other opportunities in marketing through digital technology, partnering with start-ups for developing mobile apps to drive impulse purchases.

The opportunity spaces that companies define are often like a Venn diagram—overlapping and combining different mixes of the Six Sources. This is where the real definitions of opportunity emerge. Powerful, engaging, and strategic—they capture how we truly bring together the needs and wants of markets with the technologies, brands, business models, and organizational innovations that will satisfy them, surrounded by the conditions across the ecosystem that favor the two coming together. Defining our opportunity spaces holistically— bringing together the push and pull tensions with the potential synergies—creates a strategic direction on which to focus our energy for growth.

OPPORTUNITY THINKING

Naming territories leads to claiming territories.

Our opportunities cascade from inspiring territories to actionable spaces.

Opportunities are different for every company because the value they can create is unique.

BIG
STARTERS

Opportunity starters

A pinch of pepper launched an enormous opportunity! Spices were in great demand in the 1400s, as anyone who had eaten the food would attest to. The rich used to wear a bag of pepper on their belts to signify their wealth. That may seem strange unless you know that an ounce of pepper could be traded evenly for an ounce of gold; nothing to sneeze at!

Trading of spices goes back thousands of years. Arab nations traded with Venice, giving the Venetians a European monopoly much to the consternation of their neighbors. But then something really big happened. It didn't look much like the start of an opportunity at the time, but it was certainly the spark that lit things up. The Ottoman Turks cut off overland trade in 1453, monopolizing and charging a premium for goods and inadvertently starting a firestorm of efforts in maritime trade.

The Portuguese led the way. Vasco da Gama's navigation of the Cape of Good Hope and successful trip to India in 1498 opened the sea route for trading and significant financial rewards for the Portuguese. The Portuguese so dominated that the Spanish scurried to find a trade route of their own, preferably one that didn't create direct conflict with their neighbor. Ferdinand Magellan led a voyage in 1520 opening the first westward route to Asia, naming the Pacific Ocean (peaceful ocean) and becoming the first expedition to circumnavigate the world.

Opportunity started in many places: a pinch of pepper; a big headache from the Ottoman Turks; competitors in the form of Venetians and Portuguese; new technologies to see farther, map better, and gain greater insight; and a wide open ocean.

In hindsight these opportunities look obvious—a nice linear story from history that tells us how it all came about. Just like the dozens of business cases that we have all read, they sound easy, even obvious, and we wish it could be us. But opportunity is rarely that obvious. By the time an opportunity is evident it will be amass with competitors. New opportunity is something we must search for. We need to comb through our opportunity finders, and find the pieces that will kick-start something big.

The way we find the starting place for opportunity is again similar to how we begin putting the pieces of a puzzle together. We have made piles within piles, congregating pieces we think will match. And now it's time to really get going. We find a special piece to start with, one with a distinctive feature: the bright mast of the boat, a sunlit roof, a flower that is crisply defined in a blur of blooms. And we build off of it. We look for connections—colors and shapes that match. We put our first two pieces together and it cascades from there. More matches of color and shape. As we work, the picture becomes clearer. Soon we have our section done! The space is defined.

In piecing together opportunities we, too, will often see something distinctive as we gather our trends, explore our dimensions, and probe for insights. A big Aha!— something that hits us as ripe for opportunity. These are the exciting nuggets that inspire us to search for gold. They grab our attention and start our imagination running. Such big Ahas are our Opportunity Starters. Perhaps a seed trend—something little that may be set to grow. Maybe it's a white space we found when stretching a dimension or perhaps it is an insight from an unusual user. How about a new technology or business model that could be imported to create new value. These are all exciting and suggest opportunity that may be emerging.

Opportunity doesn't reside only in the new, the small, the white space, or the unusual. Opportunity can be overlooked at the other extreme: something old rather than new, something big and even obvious rather than little, a completely black space rather than a white space, or something ubiquitous rather than unusual.

There are many possible opportunity starters. We explore a few in an industry that has long been thought difficult for innovation—healthcare. Healthcare is known to hold huge opportunities, but defining them and picking where to play is challenging because while there are staggering needs there are also overwhelming costs and issues of scale.

New

Change is an author of opportunity. Truly new things are always worth a closer look. New patents, opinion leaders, companies, products, changes in regulation, and evolving behaviors all signal the potential for growth. Sometimes the new thing may come from an adjacent industry, such as the advent of smart technologies that are showing up just about anywhere.

A new solution

One of the challenges with healthcare is that it requires we cooperate. Many of us may know what we are supposed to do in the arena of exercising but either don't do it or do it incorrectly, causing more harm than good. Now a Finnish company, Myontec, is trying to give us a helping hand. They have embedded sensors in athletic clothing that can tell us how hard different muscle groups are working and even subtly nudge us in the right direction. They are even exploring opportunities in encouraging desk-bound office workers to be more active, poking and prodding people to get up and move around.

A Dutch firm, Philips, is also working to create better health in the workplace through their computer monitors! The Ergosensor monitor can detect posture, neck position, and so forth, and give feedback to sit up straighter, adjust viewing distance, or get up and take a walk.

Old

While opportunity from the new seems obvious, we might not expect to find it in the old. But then that is precisely why we should look there! Perhaps people have tried and failed in the past, or perhaps the solutions that exist look adequate and have not been challenged.

An old package

🌳 Consider the ho-hum prescription pill bottle. The only advance for years was the development of child-proof caps. But the number of prescriptions issued worldwide is on the rise, with the main consumers being an increasingly older population. Herein lies a trifecta of challenges—more prescriptions per person, combined with poor eyesight and some cognitive challenges, leads to mix-ups in medication, resulting in serious health issues. Deborah Adler, a master's student in design, saw the problem firsthand when her grandmother inadvertently took the wrong medicine and became ill. She examined a pill bottle and found a myriad of ways to improve its design. She flipped it upside down, made the bottle flat so there was more space for printing larger type and developed wide necks with interchangeable colored rings to make prescriptions appear different. Target, a U.S. retailer, saw the opportunity and worked with Adler to get the bottle approved by the U.S. Food and Drug Administration and to integrate it into all aspects of their supply chain. Since then Target's pharmacy business has experienced double-digit growth. Adler and team won the Industrial Design Society of America's gold award and Design of the Decade for the first decade of the 21st century. A big idea, the pill bottle points to an even bigger opportunity—the need for more elderly-friendly packaging across all product categories, an opportunity that few companies have really embraced. Who would have thought it would be addressed in healthcare first? 🌳

White space

White spaces are places where there is a lack of competiton. They could exist because no one has come up with a viable offer or because no one has stretched to see the opportunity. Of course, the absence of competitors might mean it is a dead zone with no real demand, but the white space at least flags potential. These spaces may be obvious as we map existing offers along our opportunity dimensions, or they may emerge as we extend the endpoints of the dimensions to see new space or stretch to see space between current offers.

An empty space

❡ A rapidly aging population globally is putting pressure on housing for the elderly. In developing nations the majority of elderly live with family. In developed nations the majority do not live with children, and many live alone, oftentimes widowed. Yet more recently in countries with faster growing economies such as Japan, the Republic of Korea, and Thailand, attitudes have been changing. Children are less likely to see themselves as responsible for the care of their parents, and the parents are more eager for independence and privacy. How have developed nations dealt with this?

For decades, the options for senior citizens who could no longer fully care for themselves were limited to living with family or in a nursing home. But times changed. Seniors are remaining more active and don't want to give up their social circles. The limited options no longer meet the needs of seniors—if they ever did. There was a significant white space between living with relatives and living in a nursing home. New offers emerged for assisted living communities. Facilities now offer a range of assistance levels that allow the resident to stay connected with friends despite some diminishing capabilities. This opportunity has grown to include various levels of semi-independence, such as in-home nursing and communal retirement complexes. There are even specialty communities such as golf communities or houseboats. The market in the United States alone is already worth $40 billion and is expected to double by 2030 as more boomers retire. The opportunity will grow in both developed and developing nations and is now extending to entire cities where they are exploring new approaches to urban planning that are more elderly friendly. ❡

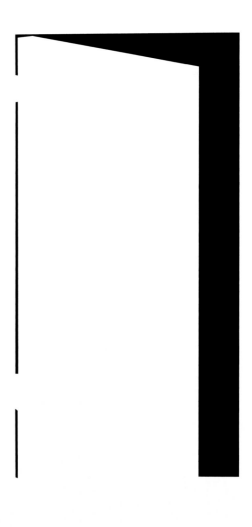

Black space

If an area devoid of competition is white, then one swarming with competitors is starting to darken. This unattractive space gets even darker when an industry has high entry costs, is in maturity, and is increasingly consolidated. But what appears as black can often have its own white spaces. We may think it is a black space because we are looking only at the traditional industry dimensions. Look at the same space along different opportunity dimensions, and there may be no competition at all. This happens when we go beyond stretching dimensions, which may have long been stretched too far, and instead move out along an entirely different dimension than those traditionally used. Thus even the blackest of spaces can be attractive if we imagine entirely new dimensions.

A crowded space

The medical device market is a crowded space. Several large suppliers, such as GE Healthcare (UK), Medtronic, and Boston Scientific, and a few niche players such as Cadwell Labs vie for ever-shrinking pots of money in developed nations where there is a lot of pressure to reduce healthcare costs. Innovation is slowing, and new products are largely evolutionary rather than revolutionary. Decisions are often made on the basis of cost. Development times are long because of regulatory pressures. While the markets are growing due to an aging population, the growth is not as strong as in years past. Meanwhile in developing nations, most healthcare providers simply cannot afford the expensive equipment marketed in Europe and the United States and often opt for lower tech, homegrown solutions.

Despite the constraints, GE Healthcare decided to target developing markets. They approached several different dimensions at once—market focus, engineering, development time, cost, and business model. Engineers took a 15-pound electrocardiograph (ECG) machine and squeezed it into a portable device that can be held with one hand. They developed it in 18 months for 60% of the cost, using off-the-shelf parts. The MAC 400 costs $1,500, instead of $10,000 for a conventional ECG machine. But it would have failed had they sold it through normal channels. So they built onto their idea a new business model and go-to-market strategy. They worked with the State Bank of India, leveraging their penetration in rural areas, and provided no-interest loans to rural doctors. Doctors would be able to pay for the machine in only two years, charging only 50 rupees ($1) per patient. More recent versions have moved the operating cost down to 10 rupees per patient. They have now sold it in more than 100 other countries, and their goal is to develop over 100 new healthcare innovations that will reduce costs and increase access. Their approach to innovation will continue to expand the opportunity potential in medical devices in both developing and developed nations.

Little

Big opportunities often start out as something little. Perhaps it is a weak signal of change, a seed trend, or a small start-up with a new approach to an old problem. Maybe it's an inkling we have about something—an observation that we make. After all, a lot of scientific discoveries start as little observations. Little things can slip by us, like a needle in the haystack, especially if we are looking for the hay harvest. They may be observed by, well, the observant. When considered in greater depth they may point to something with growth potential.

A little observation

Zia Cristi's plastic retainer was not working well. Kelsey Wirth, a fellow MBA student at Stanford, hated wearing braces in high school. Together they wondered whether there was a smarter way to straighten teeth. What if you could make a better retainer by using advances in 3-D imaging software and then use these retainers to replace braces? In 1997 they leveraged digital imaging to create a series of clear plastic mouthpieces, molded every few weeks, that move teeth gradually. They started a company called Align Technology and launched the product Invisalign. The product delivers better aesthetics, comfort, ability to eat, less pain, and fewer gum issues. By 2012 Align Technology had over 71,000 trained providers, $2 billion in sales and 1.8 million patients served.

Two students who were not even in the dental field had a little idea that uncovered a large opportunity in the orthodontics market and disrupted the big players. As with most opportunities, other companies followed suit, developing aesthetically pleasing orthodontic solutions. Most notable was incumbent 3M who introduced ceramic brackets that blend with the color of teeth. But Align Technology was the first to develop and widely advertise products specifically for improved look and feel, taking a little idea and launching a big opportunity.

Big

Big things would seem an obvious place for opportunity—staring us in the face. But big can mean daunting, insurmountable, and end up eventually being ignored in order to focus on the manageable. A big need or pain point that goes unaddressed for years eventually becomes like the elephant in the room. Everyone assumes it is a fact of life, not sure what can be done about it. The sheer magnitude of the problem means that someone will eventually address the issue, and the solution will likely be an entirely new approach.

Too big of a need

One hundred years after heart surgery's beginning, only 10% of the people in the world can afford it. So what can one doctor do about such a massive challenge? Dr. Devi Shetty was the top heart surgeon in India in the 1990s. He was in the middle of surgery one day when he was asked to make a house call. After declining, he was persuaded that this house call could change his life. It did. The visit was to Mother Teresa. Her life inspired him to create a hospital to deliver care to those with need, not those who could afford to pay. Fifteen years later he now runs the world's largest cardiac hospital, located in Bangalore. They charge, on average, less than $2,000 per open heart surgery, a third of the price elsewhere in India and virtually nothing compared with $20,000 to $100,000 in the United States. In addition, he has grown the operation to over 35 acres of facilities for trauma and cancer care as well as hospitals in 14 other cities in India. Their telemedicine practice extends to 100 facilities in India and 50 more in Africa. With deployment of more than 5,000 dialysis machines, they now will be the largest kidney care provider in the country. They have even created an insurance program in partnership with the government.

How have they done it? They created opportunity by innovating within their organization—efficiency measures; Lean practices; training their own physicians; division of labor; daily metrics on the number of stitches, blood usage, and procedures; and balancing patient loads between those who can and those who cannot pay. The result is that they are more profitable than the average hospital in the United States, even after they give away 60 procedures a week.

Dr. Shetty's organization, Narayana Hrudayalaya, Sanskrit for "God's compassionate home," has uncovered a big opportunity through a new way to deliver value to the massive need in India, Africa, and other developing nations. And all inspired by a single motto he has on his wall:

Hands that sew are holier than lips that pray.

Mother Teresa, saint and humanitarian

Unusual

Unusual users and unusual uses signal places where there may be need that previously hasn't been seen. We often overlook people or behaviors because they are anomalies, while we focus on finding segments of customers big enough to support our business. After all, none of us wants to develop endless offers for countless niche markets. Looking at unusual users doesn't need to lead to smaller opportunities. Instead, these anomalies can help us see something our competition has not seen, pointing us to unarticulated needs across the larger market.

An unusual patient

A community hospital was seeking to increase the number of women choosing them for giving birth. They were going to survey women as to why they had chosen their hospital, but they knew they would hear the same old answers. Women choose a hospital close to them or the one their doctor is loyal to. So instead they pinpointed a tiny minority of unusual patients—women who lived far from the hospital and had a doctor that was not loyal. When asked individually why they chose the hospital, the women said the Catholic hospital's identity mattered to them. The surprising finding, though, was that these women were not Catholic and even described themselves as not being affiliated with a religion! Rather, they believed that bringing life into the world was an inherently spiritual event, not just a medical procedure. They felt that a religious hospital would celebrate the spiritual aspect of the experience.

While interesting, the question then was whether this attribute of the hospital was important to a wider market. It was! A large portion of expecting mothers yearned for a richer experience than what most hospitals provided. Even more surprising was that this attitude was then found across other services. From pediatrics to rehabilitation, services that were less technical were singled out by patients as services where they wanted more care for the emotional, psychological, or spiritual aspects of the person.

The hospital seized the opportunity. They refocused their investments so they were no longer competing head-to-head on technology and started building their unique positioning. They created prayer booklets for each month of a baby's gestation and told stories of the bells that sounded at each birth, the tales of their care givers, and special programs to uplift and encourage. Their differentiated strategy provided dramatic profit increases after years of decline.

The opportunity uncovered was even larger than in this single community. Healthcare providers have been creating new services, writing books, offering seminars, and creating companies specifically focused on the nontechnical ways to provide care and advance healing.

Ubiquitous

The ubiquitous is all around us, everywhere we look, but sometimes it is also everywhere we overlook. It's not the elephant in the room, like the big unmet needs, it's the gnat—almost imperceptible. These everyday needs are often hard to see because they are so commonplace. Perhaps they are unspoken worries, inconveniences we all must deal with; not seen as worth even mentioning, they go unstated.

The most common of problems

What could be more ubiquitous than bacteria? They are everywhere. Until relatively recently the problem had gone largely unnoticed by companies. Hand sanitizer was patented in 1966 by a student in medical school. For 20 years it remained an alien substance, relegated to institutions such as hospitals. When Gojo released the first commercial hand sanitizer, market response was lukewarm. But with each ascending epidemic scare from SARS to the Swine Flu, little bottles of gel and bulky wall

dispensers gained traction. When a study reported that sanitizer use lowered superbug outbreaks at hospitals, sales soared for Gojo's Purell brand. The opportunity was big. Other brands entered the market from Clorox's naturally oriented Burt's Bees to Germ X. New forms emerged including foams, wipes, and soaps.

With consumer awareness of germs at an all-time high, consumer goods giant SC Johnson has promoted antibacterial benefits in many of their cleaning products from their Scrubbing Bubbles line through to Pledge furniture polish. Georgia Pacific has attacked germs in public through efforts to create a touch-free restroom. They have engineered enMotion dispensers that sense your hand and deliver soap, sanitizer, or towels without even touching the device.

Hand sanitizers seem obvious in retrospect, but it took a small company from the outside, not the expected players of Procter & Gamble or Unilever, to grasp this opportunity.

Plenty of places to start

There are many more sparks that can start an opportunity. We might see opportunity by noting divergent perspectives or perhaps the rare phenomenon of consensus. There is opportunity in consolidation and in fragmentation, in things near in and things far out. Opportunities are often started at the extremes.

Whatever our opportunity starter and no matter how exciting it is, it is just like that one distinctive puzzle piece that gets us moving—a bit lonely on its own. It needs to be connected to other pieces of the puzzle for its distinctive nature to make sense. But how often have companies assumed their opportunity starters to be the alpha and omega of opportunity—the beginning and the end? They find a big need, a new technology, or an innovative business model and charge off to capture the opportunity without getting the full picture of its nature. The opportunity starter is only one piece of the puzzle of growth potential. To understand the full picture we need to complete the picture.

OPPORTUNITY THINKING

Opportunities start in unexpected places—if they were obvious they would have already been seized.

To find new opportunities we look for sparks throughout our Opportunity Finders.

Uncovering opportunity requires observing what others have overlooked.

BIG SHAPERS

Maritime trade is all good and well, assuming you have something to trade. Asia had what Europe wanted—spices and silk. But Europe was running short on what Asia wanted—silver and gold. The Dutch and the English were in particularly bad shape because they didn't have the natural reserves of precious metals. Trade imbalances were becoming a real headache. Eventually the Dutch East India Company figured out a way to solve the problem—inter-Asia trade. The missing piece in the puzzle had been Japan. The Dutch built a strong, exclusive, and long-lasting relationship with Japan, who had historically remained closed to the rest of Asia. Japan wanted western technology such as the musket, as well as the science and inventions of the Renaissance. The Dutch traded these for copper, silver, and gold from Japan and then traded these metals within India and China for silk, cotton, porcelain, textiles, pepper, and spices, which were then shipped back to Europe. They created a new business model, becoming the first multinational organization, establishing several regional headquarters. The result? They sent twice the ships and carried back five times the goods from Asia as their next competitor, the British East India Company; and they generated more than 18% in dividends for over 200 years straight. The pieces of the puzzle were there all along, but the Dutch put them all together.

While opportunity lies within each Source, big opportunity comes when we connect them.

The definition of opportunity as one of relationship tells us that we need to look beyond the individual Sources to how they might interact. We can shape opportunity by how we put the pieces together.

Let's return to our puzzle for a bit more insight. With a distinctive puzzle piece in hand, we look for colors and patterns that match, knobs and notches that might fit together. We are looking for connection to other pieces. In opportunity shaping, the need is like the notch in the puzzle piece. The ability to create value is like the knob that fits into that notch, and the matching colors and patterns of the pieces are like the conditions that allow the two to come together in a meaningful way.

In the trickiest of puzzles there may be several pieces that fit together but their patterns don't match. And there will be patterns that match, but the pieces don't interlock. Opportunity landscaping can also get a bit tricky at times. We might have a market need and a technology solution but fail to see that the culture and other aspects of the environment aren't favoring the two coming together. Or we may have the perfect conditions for value to meet need but fail to realize that we don't have the right technology platforms. Just as with a puzzle—it isn't done until the pieces fit together and the patterns align.

Shaping opportunities is the active process of defining both what the opportunity can be and what we can be to the opportunity.

We are opportunity shapers!

There is one aspect in which making a puzzle is different from piecing together our opportunities. In opportunity landscaping we are not handed a puzzle that someone else created. Instead, we are both puzzle creator and puzzle maker. We make the puzzle by discovering how pieces fit together. But we can also influence the actual shape of the pieces and help engineer how they fit together. After all, we are not an outside observer of the opportunity landscape; we are participants in the opportunity ecosystem.

We are the potential creators of value, the awakeners of needs, and the participants and influencers of the conditions that define opportunity.

We can't magically evoke needs where they don't exist, defy the laws of physics to create new technologies, leap over competitors with a single bound, or circumvent regulations we find bothersome. But we can help shape the landscape and the opportunities within it through our own inventiveness and imagination. The Six Sources enable us to both discover the shape of and to actively shape opportunities. Once we have a starter

in hand we turn to each of the Six Sources to see how we can stretch the opportunity, overcome any stifling influences, support it, and ultimately sustain it. In doing so we are actively shaping our destinies.

Stretching and supersizing

If we have a spark of an opportunity it only makes sense that we would want to fan it into a fire. We do this by examining each of the Sources to see how they might help us. A new technology may be a good start, but what if we come up with an inexpensive way to manufacture it? This could make the technology accessible to a much larger audience, expanding the opportunity further. Or perhaps we complement that technology with amazing ergonomic design, improving its ultimate usability, elevating the technology and experience, and, in turn, stretching the opportunity for ourselves and likely others.

If our opportunity starter is a market need, we might look to a business model to create tiered offers that increase the size of the market. If our starter is a new brand position, we might look to the environment to develop even greater advocacy and dialogue to give the brand greater traction.

Shaping and stretching opportunity is like blowing up a balloon. Each Source we use is like a puff of fresh air—it expands and stretches, shaping the opportunity and making it bigger.

Opportunity doesn't arrive on our doorstep, fully formed.

We are the shapers of opportunity and our destinies.

In some cases we will find that what looked like a stretcher could actually be a supersizer. Supersizing occurs when the stretching Source surpasses even the original opportunity starter in its brilliance.

🌲 For Invisalign, Cristi and Wirth could have simply introduced their product to the current orthodontics market. Instead they supersized the opportunity by going after a largely untapped market: adults. The big insight was that many adults wanted straight teeth but inwardly reeled at the idea of looking like a 12-year-old. Braces conjured up memories of kids being called names— brace face, metal mouth, or tinsel teeth! Targeting adults created new potential for doctors as well as generated greater pull for the innovation. Align Technology further stretched the opportunity with their business model. They secured investment from Silicon Valley that allowed them to expand rapidly, launching an aggressive direct-to-consumer advertising campaign. The campaign created a groundswell of demand that had long been pent up. 🌲

Stifling

As we seek to stretch opportunity, Source by Source, we likely will come across issues that will stifle, stunt, or even stop it in its tracks. Perhaps there is a technical hurdle that must be overcome or the opportunity will be dead in the water. Maybe there is an impending regulation that will be tough to meet. The issue could be bad timing—the economy crashes or consumers aren't ready. If we look carefully we will see that almost every opportunity has at least one Achilles' heel—something that will be its downfall if not addressed. Identifying this early helps us innovate and strategize against it, or come to the conclusion that the issue is a deal breaker.

🌳 In the case of Invisalign, overcoming a stifler was, in fact, the spark that lit the opportunity; namely, that the aesthetics of braces had long stifled demand among adults. But there were other potential stiflers: the orthodontic community for one. Orthodontists had been educated about traditional alignment methods, with which they were very satisfied. The learning curve for an already busy and highly lucrative professional was a barrier to adoption. They would have to have incentives to learn, and it would need to be easy. So Align built a business model that created a premium product for doctors to sell but also reduced staff time by largely automating the process. They started an educational arm of the company, becoming both trainer of newly licensed Invisalign providers and tracker of newly fitted Invisalign patients. All these efforts overcame the challenges of introducing a medical technology. 🌳

Sometimes the Achilles' heel of opportunity is our own organization. Opportunity requires change, and change can be tough. Brand managers have short stints and often cannot afford to pursue opportunities that are over the horizon. R+D may resist change due to the lack of cross-functional interest, which can translate into years of projects that don't make it to market. Perhaps the opportunity withers due to our very own sales force, which finds it easier to sell large volumes of products than to introduce new products that will be niche for a while. True, these are largely executional issues, but they influence our ability to create the right value at the right time. And our ability to create value is one-third of the opportunity equation. An opportunity that looks appealing in theory can be hard to pursue in practice.

Recognizing stiflers and stoppers early can be one of the keys to unlocking and shaping opportunity. If we can overcome them we may be able to capitalize on an opportunity that has been attacked by many but never conquered.

Supporting

When one of the Six Sources cannot be used to stretch and is not likely to stifle, it may play a more humble role: that of supporting the opportunity. Perhaps the industry infrastructure has excess capacity that is sufficient to meet the demands of new opportunity. The current business models, brands, technologies, or even market segments may match the needs of the opportunity. These Sources will do nicely aligning with the opportunity. But just because a Source plays a supporting role, its potential contribution to growth should not be ignored. These functions can enhance opportunity further with a bit of tweaking. Brand positions may need to be refined, designs refreshed, and communications renewed. The opportunity may be best served through incremental improvements to assets, processes, and business systems.

🌱 Align supported their opportunity through the development of an information technology (IT) infrastructure that made it easy for doctors, because Align managed and stored all the images. Sitting quietly behind the scenes, IT was not seen as the big innovation. But it may end up being big as it now houses the largest database of tooth movements in the world, leading Align to develop services for ongoing education and software, and new imaging techniques and scanners.

The organization has continued to evolve to support the growth of the opportunity, adding distribution partners along the way, staffing up around the world, and expanding their internal training.🌱

Sustaining

Shaping an opportunity is not just a matter of stretching it for today. It is a matter of stretching it into the future. One thing we know about opportunities is that they are always on the move. Our exploration of them should include which paths they are likely to take. **When we track where an opportunity is going, we can develop the opportunity road map.** In this way we predict whether the growth we hope to achieve will be really sustainable. The best opportunities are those that are sustainable across the triple bottom line of profit, planet, and people. We start by looking at profits and then turn our attention to the planet and people. We do this not because we are greedy or care less for people and the planet, but because if an opportunity cannot sustain profits it should not even be pursued. Such an opportunity will hardly provide the resources needed to be good stewards of people and the planet.

So we check out just how long this opportunity can generate revenue by trying to build road maps across the Six Sources. Let's imagine the variety of brand positions that fit with the opportunity both now and into the future, how price could evolve, what segments can be targeted and stretched into, how capacity and infrastructure might change, the likely evolution of technologies, and the future of regulation. Opportunity road maps help us prevent a cycle of brand extensions that cannibalize each other. They help us avoid the quicksands of margin erosion. They reveal when technology will be obsolete or when capacity investments are likely to be needed. The exercise of creating an opportunity road map will be imperfect but it will illuminate another aspect of the opportunity—its depth. Road maps show us if there is really a runway for growth to be sustainable. Not all opportunities we choose to pursue will be sustainable. One-hit wonders can create exciting new growth. But we really need to know the difference between these and sustainable opportunities to prevent tricking ourselves into thinking we can get big sustainable growth when the opportunity is nothing more than an idea.

If you want to hit the ground running, you better grab your opportunity road map.

🌳 Align Technology didn't stop at making a big splash in the orthodontics market. In a risky move, they have sustained their opportunity and their growth by expanding the offer beyond orthodontists to general practitioner dentists. Now dentists can take orthodontic cases and increase their revenues. Align further engaged the external ecosystem by working to add their method to the curriculum of dental schools in 2003. In 2008 they extended their growth by targeting a new segment—teens—a group that clearly has their own aesthetic concerns. The technology road map has included growing their digital, software, and scanning products. In addition they have added new technical features that allow the product to be used on more difficult cases. They have added the ability to affix tiny permanent nobs onto a tooth here or there. The retainers can grasp these harder-to-move teeth, making Invisalign appropriate for cases that would have been relegated to using traditional braces. 🌳

Thinking about opportunity road maps prepares us for taking a longer view of sustainability for the planet and people. We can plan our technology and infrastructure road map to be sustainable environmentally. Our long-term business model can incent our partners, customers, and consumers to help us reclaim resources. Our brand can tell a story of sustainability and subtly put pressure on our competitors to meet or exceed our standards. Our organizations can participate in fair labor practices and source products from others who do the same. We can band together with the influencers and opinion leaders in our environment to create programs that will benefit our communities. Our ability to shape the opportunity into a sustainable one for people and planet, now and in the future, must serve as a criteria for selecting or deselecting opportunities to pursue.

OPPORTUNITY THINKING

We can shape our future, because we can shape our opportunities.

The Six Sources become our opportunity stretchers, supersizers, and sustainers.

Opportunity roadmaps give us the long view of opportunity so we don't chase ones that are short-lived.

BIG STORIES

We have all heard of fish stories. Fishermen are notorious for returning with tall tales of their catch or the one that got away. Every tale has two parts—the size of the fish and the story behind it.

Explorers had similar tales. Stories of riches and their abundance were told to entertain, impress, and most often to secure funding for future voyages. Their stories were critical for their own success, the success of their investors, and for expansion of the world in general.

Opportunity tales are similar. They tell of the size and nature of the opportunity, and they are meant to persuade our organizations to invest and launch new endeavors. Getting an accurate understanding of the nature of an opportunity can be challenging though. Companies will often estimate the market potential of an individual product concept but struggle to assess the nature and potential for all the offers that might exist in the opportunity. So how do we size and describe opportunities in a way our organizations will believe and invest in?

Sizing opportunities

⚓ Let's take a look at the biggest sizing story to emerge from the endeavors of explorers, mathematicians, and cartographers alike—the size of the earth itself.

Plato (400 BC) estimated a circumference of 40,000 miles; Archimedes (250 BC) said 30,000. Eratosthenes (200 BC) was getting very close with figures between 25,000 and 28,000. Posidonius was in the ballpark as well, thanks to some errors that canceled out. He said it was 24,000 miles. Later, Ptolemy (200 AD) said 18,000. While Eratosthenes' and Posidonius' estimates were closest to the actual circumference of 24,900, the value that was used by explorers in the 1400s was Ptolemy's smaller estimate because his writings got picked up by the scholars of the time. As a result, there were some poorly planned trips and some very hungry crew members. Columbus thought his trip would only be a few thousand miles. Magellan thought the voyage would take weeks when it was months, leading starving sailors to eat whatever they could find to survive. ⛵

Sizing opportunities is equally tricky business. Like Plato, they can start out too big and then shrink with time. Estimates may begin as overconfident or oversimplistic back-of-the-envelope calculations based on looking only at the size of a market. After all, if we just got 1% of the market in China—the opportunity would be huge! Of course, we are only one of thousands of other companies who hope to capture 1% and the numbers just don't add up!

We can also, like Ptolemy, underestimate the size of an opportunity, leaving our organization unprepared for its magnitude and starving for resources. Perhaps our organization lacks vision for just how big the opportunity really is, looking only at the market and ignoring the other Sources and their power to stretch and supersize. Underestimating can lead us to underresourcing opportunities, eventually ceding them to hungrier competitors willing to stock up for the full journey.

Of course, sometimes an opportunity looks small, because we think ourselves too big for it. Ptolemy's estimates of the earth's size remained for years until Gerardus Mercator (1512–1594), a Flemish cartographer, reduced the size of Europe and the Mediterranean —effectively increasing the size of the earth. Big companies regularly underestimate the long-term value of an opportunity because they overestimate their own size and importance. Opportunities most companies would be pleased with are too small for the big kids on the block, and they end up missing out on much growth as a result.

Not accurately understanding the size of an opportunity can hurt us in many ways—we either won't go on the journey or we won't be prepared for the journey we go on.

Our appreciation for the size of an endeavor unfolds as we explore it. Just like when doing a puzzle—we see how big it really is as we put the pieces together. It's the same with opportunity. The more we work at it, the more we can appreciate its magnitude. Shaping opportunities gives us a unique perspective on their size, helping us to remember that the size will change for a company with different capabilities. Opportunity sizing goes beyond estimating the size of the market to taking into consideration how we are going to shape, supersize, and sustain the opportunity. Our potential activities across all the Sources tell the story about its possibilities.

Many wrongs make a right.

Ecosystem sizing

Shaping opportunities also tells us we are not alone. There is a big opportunity ecosystem waiting out there to potentially partner or promote the endeavor. This ecosystem has insights on the future of the opportunity. We can go beyond asking questions of customers to estimate market potential, and turn to the opportunity ecosystem to get their view. And they like to talk! Pursuing multiple perspectives is a way of accessing the wisdom of crowds. It's been shown that individuals cannot predict with accuracy the number of jelly beans in a jar, but, despite this, the average of the guesses taken across a group typically will be correct. The errors cancel each other out. So it is with the ecosystem. If we ask enough of these visionaries, perhaps biased in their own right, together they will provide a sense of the real proportions.

In addition to getting a better sense of the whole opportunity, the ecosystem helps us understand the individual drivers of size and how to make the potential even bigger. Technologists predict growth through the lens of adoption curves and product life cycles. Brand experts and retailers predict based on how long it takes to grow new brands and how big they become. Designers understand how long it takes for things to catch on, spread, or die out. Cultural critics and observers think about the time and influences necessary to change behaviors and how those behaviors spread. Financial analysts speak to total market size and reflect on competitive position and potential. One person will think of opportunity size in shelf space, another in intellectual property, one in units shipped, and another in margins; one person will reflect on the preferences of individuals and another on preferences of communities.

⚓ Multimethod approaches to sizing are not new. Over time many people in many places developed a variety of methods to estimate the earth's size. The Indian mathematician Aryabhata (476–550 AD), a team of Islamic scholars sponsored by al-Ma'mun in 830 AD, and a Persian 17-year-old named Biruni (978–1048 AD) measured distances, climbed mountains, traversed deserts, watched the sun, created correction factors, and all arrived at almost perfectly accurate estimates of circumference. In doing so each advanced understanding of the nature and dimensions of both earth and stars. ⚓

Taking an ecosystem-based approach to sizing an opportunity provides more than a single number of market potential. It helps complete the story of the opportunity. Shaping the opportunity is part of the story; sizing it through the Six Sources provides the metrics of success. Unraveling these success factors helps us further strategize to stretch the opportunity, making it bigger along each of the measures used by the ecosystem.

Opportunity stories

⚓ Believe it or not, it was a bit of a fish story that raised curiosity about lands to the north. The fishermen in the British Isles were always in search of a good spot for cod. They went farther and farther west, having heard tales of Hy-Brasil, Gaelic for Isle of the Blessed, lying off the coast of Ireland. It was John Cabot who landed the big catch. In the 1490s he was sponsored by King Henry VII and began his journeys. He eventually found Newfoundland. His crew reported back that the trees were tall enough to make fine masts, and the sea was so full of fish that they could be caught by simply lowering a basket into the water. Cabot reportedly told the king that England would no longer need Iceland for their cod. The discovery produced a salary for Cabot and funding of subsequent voyages.

The age of exploration was an age of stories—stories that launched journeys and stories that came back from them. After all, imagine going to the crown to ask for a bit of gold to take a journey somewhere, to hop in your ship and take off—letting the winds guide you—because you had a hunch there were riches out there. You probably wouldn't be invited back to court.

Explorers pitched their expeditions using the very best maps, the most recent insights from others' journeys, the latest calculations of distance, a plan for the resources needed, and the returns expected. Of course, the details were still sketchy. After all, they were going somewhere new so they couldn't describe it perfectly. But they did what they could both to create a vision of what could be and to justify the funding to achieve it.

When they returned from their voyages their stories were even more colorful, describing new places, people, plants, animals, and riches. Their accounts were printed and reprinted in the thousands. Maps were annotated with images of what was seen. Samples of plants and foods were brought back and carefully shared with eager audiences. Still, no amount of description could convey the volumes experienced by the explorers themselves. ⛵

We have a similar challenge once we have explored an opportunity. There are volumes of information and insights that must be captured and conveyed if we hope to have someone invest in the adventures we propose. It is difficult to assemble it all into a meaningful story. But we have an advantage—we have taken those insights and shaped them into opportunity. We have seen the connections so we can tell a more cohesive story. And we have sized the opportunity, helping us understand its drivers.

VICTORY!

We have put in place our final puzzle pieces of opportunity, having had the luxury of being both puzzle shaper and puzzle maker. We have traveled there and talked to people through our insight work. We've looked across time both past and into the future through our trends. We've dimensionalized the opportunities, visualized them on a map, and annotated with detail. The insights, trends, and dimensions tell us the who, what, where, when, how, and why of the opportunity—the rich story of opportunity.

Our story began with our exploration of the landscape, moved to defining our spaces, and then identifying opportunity starters. Opportunity took form as we stretched, supersized, worked around stiflers, supported, and planned how to sustain it. Our opportunity road maps reveal the story today and into the future. Our opportunity story is more than a business case. It paints a picture of the desires waiting to be fulfilled, the value we can create, and the conditions that might unite them across the Six Sources and time.

Now we have some choices to make. With picture in hand we can choose where we will and won't go. We can see how big new places are, what is required for success, and whether we are suited to win there. We have what we need to prioritize. Some opportunities will be obvious choices, fitting nicely with our current abilities; others will be so big and attractive that we will make the decision to grow the capabilities we need. **For each opportunity we figure out what to leverage, build, borrow, or buy.**

After all, we shouldn't be limited by our capabilities if we can build internally, borrow through open innovation, or buy through an acquisition. Some opportunities will be right for us, others won't. We can't go everywhere, win everywhere, so with stories in hand we can make choices with confidence.

Too often, organizations are handed a mere piece of the puzzle—a big opportunity starter. The starter is viewed as the story itself, as if all the other pieces are just going to fall into place. The starter becomes the basis for sizing and the rationale for how the organization can win. Leaders are asked to launch a voyage based on these scarce details. They are not provided the array of opportunities, their accompanying stories, what each will require in the way of capabilities, the road maps associated with them, and their short- and long-term potential. In order to select opportunities—to compare them against each other—we need to look at the full picture: the landscape, territories, spaces, and their stories. Otherwise our decisions will be out of context. As time goes on, we will second-guess our choices, leading to a lack of genuine commitment to the opportunities.

In order to select opportunities—to compare them against each other—we need to look at the full picture and get the travelogues, too.

LAND HO!

Growth vision

The collection of opportunities we select forms a true growth vision. It is a picture of where we will go, and the opportunity stories for each of the destinations. Such a vision is quite different from the visions organizations often roll out—a big hairy audacious goal of the growth numbers being targeted—without an accompanying vision of where we will land in the end. Vague or daunting, what is meant to inspire provides little guidance.

Imagine asking someone to do a puzzle without the box cover—just telling them the number of pieces in the pile. It is doable, but most people would find it more frustrating than rewarding. Yet this is what we are asking our organizations to do when we simply tell them the size of the opportunity while giving no sense of the beauty and grandeur of the destination.

An opportunity-based growth vision is a big story of where we will end up, the territories we will own, the spaces we will innovate in. It should inspire and rally the organization.

Employee survey after employee survey tells us that people are motivated more by intrinsic rewards than extrinsic ones—a sense of value and contribution wins out over money almost every time. Yet we try to energize our organizations with a financial vision, failing to articulate how the organization as a whole, and the individuals within it, can create new-to-the-world value, satisfy lingering needs, and foster conditions in the ecosystem that make for lasting growth—how we ourselves and our world will be transformed by the journey.

Opportunity landscaping is the basis for inspiring visions—visions that will motivate our organizations to drive growth.

An inspiring growth vision

🌳 Royal DSM—Dutch State Mining—is a €9 billion (about $12.3 billion) Netherlands-based global company that has transformed itself through an inspiring, opportunity-based, growth vision. The vision is driving focused growth grounded in key impact trends relating to their materials and life sciences businesses. Population growth, urbanization, and rising income are creating opportunities in food fortification and security. Active, healthy-aging trends globally are stimulating efforts in preventive health and pharmaceuticals. They have mapped out trends in energy for years to come, planning for a post-fossil-fuel age, leading to their efforts in materials from bio-based resources. But they are also looking at immediate issues such as ways to minimize e-waste (the afterlife of electronics) by designing for recyclability.

Mapping emerging opportunities onto their capabilities has led to identifying potential in both their life- and materials-sciences businesses as well as in the overlap. As a result they are blending together a biomedical materials business, developing everything from new body parts to new delivery mechanisms for medicines.

The triple bottom line is always on the forefront of strategy, leading them to articulate and take action against four growth pillars. First they are focusing 70% of their effort on high growth economies. Next, they are emphasizing innovation, with an exemplary record having already lightweighted planes and boats leading to faster speed from the air to the Olympics. Their sustainability emphasis is seen in their materials innovations and production practices and regularly lands them on the Dow Jones Sustainability Index. Finally, they are growing through partnerships and acquisitions, such as their purchase of Cargill's cultures and enzymes business. Throughout, they articulate their vision for their 22,000 employees—a vision focused on safety, global diversity, and high levels of engagement and job satisfaction.

They are now taking this vision public to inspire all their stakeholders through a new corporate brand and campaign—DSM: Bright Science, Brighter Living. Their strategy, based on trends, insights, and an engaging story around where they are going, is producing strong growth despite tough economic times and resulting in sales growth that has exceeded targets. 🌳

> "If you don't know where you are going, you'll probably end up somewhere else."

Lewis Carroll, mathematician, author of Alice in Wonderland

OPPORTUNITY THINKING

Opportunity stories tell us the who, what, where, when, and why of opportunity.

The size of an opportunity depends on the unique ways a company shapes it.

Opportunity-based growth visions inspire by telling our organizations the destination for growth, not just the financial targets.

CHAPTER 6

BIG
IDEAS

"In fourteen hundred ninety-two Columbus sailed the ocean blue."

You might recall learning this line from a poem when you were trying to memorize the date of Columbus's maiden voyage. You may not remember much about his subsequent adventures though. Columbus returned from trips with vivid descriptions of the land and peoples he encountered. In his letter to Luis de Santangel, one of his financial backers, he wrote of "great mines of gold and other metals" and "very wide and fertile plains" which were "rich for planting and sowing." With the letter in hand, it is not surprising subsequent voyages were funded. But this time there were some extra passengers on board—miners and farmers, not to mention some sheep, horses, and cows! After all, if it is the job of the explorer to discover new lands, it is the job of the miners and farmers to capture the value the investors are expecting.

Miners and farmers were very different in the way they captured value from the land. Miners extracted what was; farmers planted for what would be. Mining could produce immediate returns, while farming required a bit more patience. Miners' tasks started out with a bang! but became more difficult as they dug deeper to get the next bit of ore. Farmers' jobs were more challenging in the beginning—clearing the land, cultivating the soil, figuring out which crops would grow best. But over time, yields improved. Farmers stayed for years maintaining the land while miners eventually moved on, finding new veins of ore once the old ones were tapped out.

Interestingly, the governments that sponsored the famous expeditions to new lands did so because they had tapped out their mines in Europe. They couldn't go any deeper since they didn't have the technology to do so without water filling the mine. So they went in search of new mines. And while they sent farmers on subsequent journeys, they had no idea that the farmers would return even greater value than the miners in many cases. Some of the greatest wealth came from crops that were ultimately cultivated, such as cocoa and tobacco.

Opportunity mining and farming

We, too, can bring miners and farmers to the opportunity territories we discover. Both are needed to capture the full value. We mine markets we are already in as we discover still more opportunity, strengthening our presence, our brands, and our quality to extract more. Eventually though, returns diminish, we tap out our markets, and must find new potential—perhaps from taking our offers to new customers or regions.

Some opportunity spaces are suited for the opportunity farmer.

The value isn't readily available, waiting to be extracted. It must be created. The opportunity farmer learns the lay of the land, clears obstacles, and figures out which offers will grow best. Opportunity farming requires more patience as the yields start out low but, over time, increase.

Our organizations will be more comfortable with mining opportunities.

After all, we understand the returns, have the products and services in hand, and it is just a matter of enhancing offers or expanding market presence to capture what we can. But too often what looks like an opportunity for mining is actually an opportunity for farming. We are lulled into thinking that we can simply extend our current offers into new markets when, in fact, the new markets require something different—an opportunity farmer's touch; a considered approach to planting something new.

🌱 Look at the successful and unsuccessful attempts at market expansions in recent years. Companies that approached expansion with a mining mentality—taking their offers directly from developed countries into developing countries—have failed miserably. In India, where paper-thin saris are everyday wear, Whirlpool's initial washing machine introduction failed in part because it shredded thin garments. Kellogg's cold cereal didn't fare much better since breakfast is always served warm. 🌱

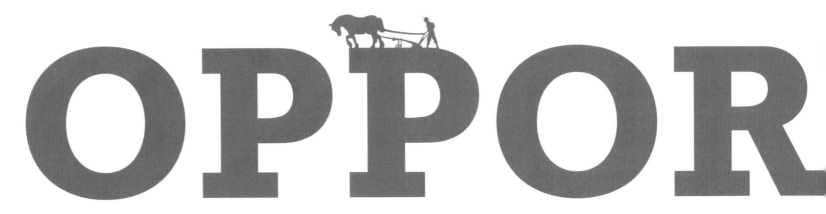

OPPOR

> " When written in Chinese the word 'crisis' is composed of two characters. One represents danger and the other represents opportunity. "
>
> *John F. Kennedy, former U.S. president*

These companies didn't study the market needs adequately and adapt their approach as a farmer would study soil and match the seed to the conditions. Many multinational companies have focused on designing for developed markets first. But increasingly companies are learning to adapt to new environments.

🌱 Initial forays of consumer goods from developing countries into emerging markets found few takers. Packages of toothpaste and shampoo were too expensive. With the realization that many laborers in emerging markets are paid daily, companies such as Colgate and Unilever found a foothold: smaller sachets with just enough for daily use and priced at the value of a coin the person was paid in.

Ethnographic research has helped companies adapt. Considerations such as shaving without water in India and washing without privacy in China became nooks and crannies to reveal the true shape of an opportunity. By studying actual needs in emerging markets, Nokia sidestepped potential flops by understanding that feature creep had little appeal to those seeking an inexpensive, sturdy cell phone. At the same time, some features were quite necessary—such as multiple contact folders for an entire family sharing one cell phone.🌱

Deciding to farm opportunities rather than mine isn't enough, though. If it was, new product introductions would be more successful. What Colgate and Unilever did was remarkably insightful, even empathetic. But not every one of our new products or services is equally well suited for our opportunities.

We need to improve our yields from opportunity farming.

TUNITY

Capturing opportunity requires both opportunity farming and mining.

Farming is planting new offers; mining is extracting value that exists.

New opportunity requires new farming methods.

BIG
FARMING

What really grew Europe? Was it exploration? Science? Art? Or the potato? The answer is more likely to be found in the humble spud. It didn't look like much when Francisco Pizarro saw Indians of South America eating it in 1532, but within a few decades Spain was growing and exporting the strange starch. Viewed as both odd and tasteless, potatoes were not widely popular right away, but over the years the rulers of several nations saw their value and encouraged people to eat them as a mainstay. The results? The potato is credited with building empires by eliminating famines occurring as frequently as every decade in Europe. The potato fueled a growing population.

Potatoes are now fueling another growing population—that of Asia. Consumption is on the rise with production in developing countries recently surpassing that of developed nations. Maybe that is why LambWeston—one of the world's largest makers of French Fries—has recently introduced Asian Moonz to fast-food chains across Asia. These small hash-brown like potato patties come in three flavors—Roasted Spring Onion, Indian Curry, and Sweet Chili—spicing up the prospects for potatoes once again.

Potatoes are a big idea! Which is surprising since they originated as a toxic root. It took the peoples of the Andes thousands of years to cultivate, eliminate toxicity, and create a range of varieties and uses.

It took hundreds more years to increase yields. Even today yields vary greatly across countries with different growing methods, with best practices producing three times as much per acre.

Wouldn't it be great if we could develop innovation practices that would increase our yields by three times? We certainly need to. The statistics described earlier are not encouraging—3,000 ideas to get something to take to the market, only half of the launches survive, and only a fraction of those produce revenue that is acceptable. Our ideas are not producing empire-building growth!

If ideas were seeds, a farmer would quit with those numbers.

Farmers have learned how to increase their yields . . . so it seems we can, too. There are a lot of similarities between farming and innovation. In both cases, something is planted and expected to grow and produce revenue. In fact, a closer look at innovation in farming practice provides a model for how we can advance innovation itself. We see four levels of innovation maturity reflected in four key advances in farming.

The evolution of farming gives us a picture of the evolution of growth itself.

Level 1: The birth of farming

Innovation in farming began like much of innovation —in a crowded place. People started out as hunters and gatherers, not hunters and farmers! But as they crowded into areas with good water, the gathering got tough and there were slim pickings. The result? People embarked on a journey of over 12,000 years of innovation to get more from the land.

Some of the earliest evidence of farming is from the Fertile Crescent in the Middle East around 9500 BC. It started simply. Gather seed from plants, toss them around and collect what grows. The method was called broadcast planting for the notion that seed was cast out broadly with the hope some would take root. And some did. But plenty didn't. Some landed on pathways, getting trampled or eaten by birds. Some landed in weedy areas where it was choked out. And some landed in rocky areas where soil was too shallow, causing early growth to die.

Sound familiar? Idea-led innovation, at its worst, is a lot like broadcast planting—cast out a bunch of ideas which turn into products that somehow get launched, only to find that too many of them fall on hard ground with no opportunity, on crowded ground of competitors, and on rocky ground of shallow demand.

This is the first level of maturity in a firm's approach to growth. At least they are trying to plant something! But the history of product failures suggests we need better targeting of our ideas . . . or else they will become nothing more than bird seed.

Case in point is the video game industry. Over 90% of video games produced do not break even. While the opportunity is large, with market estimates of over $10 billion, the majority of games are considered me-too products and are targeting either dried up or crowded places to play. There are a few big winners such as Super Mario Brothers or Halo. There are also some very successful niche players that build small franchises by finding new opportunity spaces. Japan's Square Enix did this by partnering with Disney Interactive Studios to create the Kingdom Hearts series. The series has grown to seven games across multiple consoles, selling over 17 million copies, as well as merchandise, music, figurines, novels, and a comic (Manga) series. Alternatively, most games do not share the fate of either the big players or the niche players. Instead the statistics show they are more likely to end up like some of Atari's early launches. They buried over one million games in a landfill.

Growth occurs when the right spaces are identified. The trick is to find those spaces.

Level 2: Thinking about the soil

Farmers soon figured out they could increase yields through a more methodical approach—row farming. Around 3000 BC, somewhere in China, farmers tilled the soil and created small furrows for planting. Over the years new methods were developed for analyzing and preparing the soil as well as planting at the right depths and intervals, producing even greater yields.

Our approach to opportunity landscaping provides a more methodical way to plant ideas. It takes us from broadcast seeding to soil analysis and row planting. Through careful evaluation, we pick the opportunities we want to seed with new products and services and focus only on those—avoiding the waste of going after spaces that won't reward us with growth. This is the second level of maturity in a firm's approach to growth—attention to the opportunity rather than just the ideas!

But even when we plant an idea in rich opportunity, we still aren't getting the yields we want. Competitors swoop in from behind, learn from what we've done, and capture more of the opportunity with a better crafted offer. Picking where to plant isn't enough. We've got to develop better ideas.

Latecomers Facebook and Mint both beat out the earlier entrants of MySpace and Wesabe through better interfaces, a focus on benefits rather than features, and a closer connection to what consumers wanted. Similarly late entrant Voodoo Tiki Tequila is riding on the coattails (and cocktails) of established competitor Patrón by improving on their idea. Patrón invested millions convincing people to spend big on what had traditionally been a low-end, party drink. Voodoo Tiki has entered with an even higher-end handblown glass bottle, challenging Patrón's less premium looking bottle. While companies are finding good spaces to play in, they are not always crafting the most competitive ideas or product ranges for the full opportunity.

Level 3: Thinking about the seed

🪴 Farmers decided they shouldn't be the only ones working hard—preparing soil and carefully planting. Soon the plant itself was asked to work harder. The Chinese figured out they could improve plants through grafting around 2000 BC. Grafting takes the best of different plants and merges them literally—by placing a superior part of one plant into the root or branch stock of another. The result is a stronger plant with better fruit, flower, and leaves, all creating higher yields. 🪴

While the art and science of grafting is still evolving, a new form of grafting has come on the scene—modifying seeds at a genetic level. Genetic modification combines genes from different organisms to create seeds that resist attacks from pests and produce higher yields. The science has become so sophisticated that Monsanto developed a new business model. In addition to selling seed, they license the DNA of the seed, which they own, and require the farmer to pay royalties, allowing Monsanto to share in the rewards of the crop. Today's seeds are being made to work harder. They are considered so precious they would never be scattered about as in the past!

We need to make our ideas work harder. Great products are often the combination of a great brand, a creative business model, new technology, fresh design, and a focused segmentation approach. The secret to success lies in figuring out how to graft together these parts into superstrains of ideas. Our hopes for growth ultimately lie in how well we do this.

🌳 At a time when the world is becoming more virtual than physical and consumers have greater rather than less choice, Redbox DVD kiosks came along and scooped up one-third of the market share in the United States with an offer that was both physical and offered less variety. They rent only the most popular DVD and game disks for $1 a day from any of over 40,000 kiosks. By partnering with a range of retailers rather than just one—McDonald's to Walgreens—they have managed to locate a kiosk within five minutes of over 60% of the population. Reliability has driven loyalty; regional supervisors service the kiosks, which are also supported by an IT backbone that ensures constant monitoring and uptime. They have grown both organically and through acquisition of NCR's Blockbuster-branded kiosks and are now partnering with Verizon to roll out a streaming service. 🌳

Growth doesn't come from the farmer; it doesn't come from the land. It's from the seed. Everything else is just giving the seed a chance to thrive.

Level 4: Thinking about cultivation

Despite all the advances, farmers still weren't completely happy. The bane of the farmers' existence has always been the weather. It is the pipe dream of every farmer, as well as the occasional mad scientist in movies and comic books, to control the weather. But it wasn't a mad scientist who figured out how to help farmers.

Robert Thomas published the *Old Farmer's Almanac* in 1792, a publication so insightful it still guides farmers today, making it the oldest continuously published periodical in America. Thomas studied astronomy, solar activity, and weather patterns and created a highly complex, secretive forecasting method, which brought astoundingly accurate results. So much so that the method is still guarded, reportedly hidden in a tin box somewhere in New Hampshire!

Beyond looking at the *Old Farmer's Almanac*, farmers use the latest in weather tracking in an effort to better protect and cultivate their crops. Weather satellites predict, irrigation augments, smudge pots warm orchards during late-spring frosts, and helicopters dry fruit when rain threatens to ruin the harvest. Weeds and pests are controlled and plants fertilized. Cultivation extends right down to the individual plant—hothouses germinate seeds in controlled environments, and, once planted, sprouts are carefully thinned out to provide more air flow and access to water and nutrients.

Of course, we would love to control the environment into which we launch products—masterminding cultures, regulations, competitive responses, and public opinion to favor our products. But short of that, we can influence the influencers, look out to the trends to determine timings for launches, and support our innovations better once they enter the market. We can nurture our offers in infancy, cultivating them in closed environments and later thinning out less-than-promising ones in order to pay more attention to and put greater resources toward those that are showing potential.

Nurturing is what it will take to sell personal care products into parts of Africa where the understanding of their importance has not been developed. Procter & Gamble would clearly like to be one of the market leaders when the market is ready. But in the meantime, they are in the process of creating the market. In an effort to introduce Pampers, Always, and Ariel detergent, they found a more pressing need—for clean water. They formed a nonprofit to take their PUR water purification product into Kenya. They introduced a business model that allows women to purify the water and sell it door-to-door, through kiosks, a store, and now a van. The women are also selling other P+G products. In partnership with the Kenyan government and other nonprofits, they are incentivizing women to go to clinics for delivery of their babies and antenatal care. With these efforts they are educating, saving lives, creating loyalty, and selling product in places that would otherwise be unreceptive.

Precision farming

Combining the best of advances in planting, soil, seed, and growing conditions is now called precision farming. Has it paid off? The answer is a resounding yes. In the last 50 years alone, grain yields have increased over 300% globally. Precision farming has the power to transform how the world produces food. It is not just a highly technical approach limited to developed nations; it is a growing opportunity in and of itself in developing nations.

🌱 A frugal form of precision farming is emerging in India. This lower tech version doesn't require satellites and sophisticated sensors. Instead, it focuses on simple processes and controlling costs. The majority of farmers use traditional methods such as broadcast seeding, wasting precious seed. Seeds are overwatered or underwatered; fertilizers and crop protection chemicals are overapplied, hurting soil productivity. Frugal precision farming reduces the input costs—costs of seed and fertilizers. Jain Irrigation Systems in Jaipur has developed drip systems that save money and result in more eco-friendly farming. Yields have gone from eight quintals per acre to 35 quintals per acre, a 430% increase in yield. The rise of precision farming is leading a green revolution in India and dramatically increasing wealth in many villages.🌱

We need precision farming of opportunities. Opportunity landscaping gives us a picture of the landscape and the nature of the growing conditions so we know where to plant. Now we need to use the insights we have gained through our exploration to think more deeply about the ideas to plant. We need to graft together ideas that will bear more fruit. Once we design these special strains, we will need to cultivate them so they survive and reach fruition.

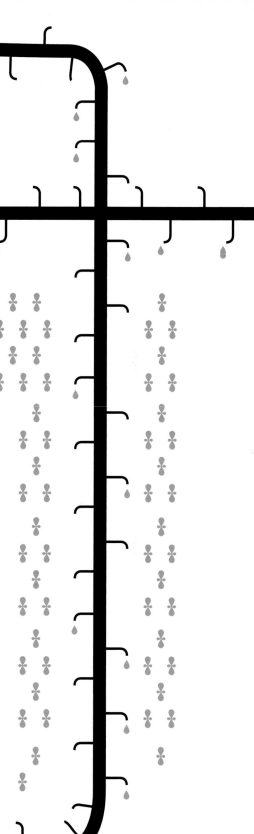

OPPORTUNITY THINKING

Getting the yields we want from an opportunity requires that we mature as opportunity farmers.

Precision farming of opportunities involves:

- landscaping our opportunities,

- picking where to farm,

- grafting together the right offers, and

- cultivating the conditions for growth.

KILLER IDEAS

Quick! Think of one of the biggest ideas ever.

Tough to choose?

While we all have our favorites, many would agree that chocolate has to be on the list! You might not have thought so though if you had tasted it in 1519 when Hernán Cortés first came across it. At the time, it was served up to Aztec rulers as a bitter, frothy drink with a bit of chili thrown in. It did not meet with rave reviews back in Spain until someone came along and mixed it with sugar and spices such as nutmeg. It was so popular the Spanish kept it a secret for almost 100 years. It became a craze in France, used in candies and seen as an aphrodisiac. In London, chocolate houses popped up where you could sip the drink with your friends. The Dutch figured out how to squeeze out the cocoa butter creating an even better drink. The English then put the cocoa butter back in, making the first chocolate bar in 1830. After years of experimentation, the Swiss finally worked out how to add in powdered milk to make milk chocolate.

Today you can buy chocolate in just about any form including bars and drinks, breakfast cereal—and even cologne. To get a taste of the varieties from around the world, you can go to the 100% Chocolate Cafe in Kyobashi, Japan, where you can taste 56 different kinds, or take a trip to the UK to try out a new 3-D printer for chocolate and create your own delicacies.

Chocolate, as experienced today, is the result of a series of innovations linked together. The original idea had the raw material of greatness but was not a big idea by itself. It's the same with most big ideas. They like company. They need to be surrounded by other ideas to shine their brightest.

A big idea is a bundle of ideas grafted together to create something altogether new, strong, and more fruitful.

The goal of opportunity landscaping is not to end up with a landscape! The goal is to end up with killer ideas that lead to growth. Rather than jump directly into idea development though, opportunity landscaping provides us with the clues we need for creating holistic ideas that will really deliver.

Grafting together ideas

Grafting together an idea that really fits an opportunity and delivers on it in a big way may sound a bit daunting—but we already have a lot of the insight needed to do so. By shaping our opportunities, we learned a lot about what might grow well in them. We have a gist of the technologies, price points, and brand positions that will fit. What we don't know is how to fine tune each of these and how to combine different ideas to create a superstrain. After all, there are hundreds, even thousands, of possibilities.

Imagine that each idea is like a point in space. If you think back to your math class, you will remember that a point can be defined by its coordinates (x, y, z) and the space is defined by the x, y, and z axes. In the same way, a product or service offering is defined by its coordinates—a specific brand, technology, business model, target market, and so on—along the axes of the opportunity space. The axes end up being the Six Sources and the opportunity dimensions within them. When we landscape the space, our opportunity cartography defines the boundaries of opportunity spaces along each dimension, telling us what's in and what's out. But even with these boundaries, there are still hundreds of points in the space, hundreds of products or service combinations possible; and it is not yet clear which will be best.

Botanists setting out to graft a better plant face a similar challenge—the possibility of hundreds of combinations. They have a variety of attributes they are looking to combine —from fruit size to quality, disease to drought resistance, hardiness of roots to stems. They narrow in on the right combination by first understanding what the environment requires and will reward. They next search for the best of the best, picking the plants that will deliver on each dimension. And finally, they explore the combinations, determining the elements that work together to create a plant that will produce a much bigger yield.

We build superstrains of ideas in a similar fashion. We start by using our opportunity landscaping to understand what the environment requires and will reward. Next, we work on the parts of the offer individually, developing the best of the best ideas within each of the Sources. Finally, we explore what combinations of these ideas complement each other.

Business leaders sometimes say, "I don't want more ideas—I want bigger ideas!"

Leaders want different kinds of ideas, the next generation of ideas very much alive and bursting with growth potential—not a one-dimensional idea but an idea that is multidimensional. These are **Big Ideas, Killer Ideas,** ideas that are engineered to reflect the nature of opportunity, intertwined bundles of ideas that form a compatible, attractive offer where the whole is greater than the sum of the parts.

Individual ideas may address unmet needs, but big ideas capture opportunities.

Big ideas can be big for many reasons. They might be big because they are enduring, lock out the competition, or deliver big revenue. Perhaps there is one really big idea—an offer that takes a more all-encompassing brand position, targets a larger swath of the market, or sets a new standard in technology. Such offers become mega-points in space—centers of gravity that result in market leadership. Other times a big idea might be a constellation of offers—a product line that represents multiple products, each of which capture a different part of the space. A really big idea will often be all of the above.

🌳 Sodastream is a big idea: a countertop system that allows consumers to make carbonated beverages at home. Simply add tap water, choose your flavor, and then the system carbonates your drink. Syrups range from colas to energy drinks, fruits to teas. The company partners with others such as Kraft to deliver favorites including Crystal Lite and Country Time Lemonade. Consumers get refills of CO_2 from a distribution center or the grocery store, saving them money and cupboard space for packaged drinks and reducing their concerns regarding the impact of packaging on the environment. The appeal is broad—broad enough to give Sodastream a market presence in over 40 countries. An acquisition of Italy's CEM Industries srl has positioned them for food service channels as well. It's a killer idea that knits together business models, brands, technologies, markets, and sustainability benefits.🌳

The Six Sources of opportunity are also the Six Sources of big ideas.

Unfortunately, building such Six-Sourced ideas doesn't come naturally. It's not how our imagination works and it follows that it's not how our idea development processes work. An idea pops into our heads, which usually fits within a single one of the Sources. It may be a stunning idea within its own rights, but what happens next is problematic. If the idea resonates within the organization it will be put into some sort of development process where it is eventually passed along to the next function. Unfortunately, a lot of the brilliance of the idea gets lost in this process. Design is dumbed down to meet price points, brand messaging fails to communicate the value of a technology, or a new business model is rolled out using old sales approaches, and it falls flat. The resulting offer looks more like the old crazy quilts made of scraps than a well-crafted work of art. Getting to bigger ideas takes more than thinking harder. It takes learning the art of grafting together truly distinctive superstrains of ideas.

Opportunity storming

Opportunity landscaping has given us a lot to work with, but the way we work will be very different from what we have been doing to date. Current ideation methods, while good at spurring creativity, don't systematically build ideas from the opportunity up. Typically, we launch creative energy from a single starting point—a big insight, trend, target market, or need. The starting point is like dropping a pebble into a pond, with rings moving outward from the center. We stretch further and further to generate new ideas, but the ripples of creativity become smaller the farther we go. We never know if we have gone as far as we can. We can't see if we have explored the whole pond or if we still have room to stretch, having tapped only one fishing hole.

What if we had a map of the pond and could pick any place in it rather than dropping a pebble in one spot? Opportunity cartography is that map. It allows us to combine points on the dimensions to choose any place in the pond. As we explore different combinations, we find entirely new ways to deliver on opportunity. Despite all the merits of creativity methods—from lateral thinking to de Bono's six hats—it is ultimately the opportunity that defines and enriches what can and should be.

Opportunity storming is an opportunity-driven ideation method that allows us to create ideas that span the full space of the opportunity. The opportunity dimensions reveal the parts of the opportunity we have overlooked. They allow us to explore the whole space, stretching beyond where we thought possible, even navigating along dimensions that will get us out of areas that have been overfished.

A new cologne

🌱 Imagine we wanted to ideate around an opportunity space for premium cologne because we seek higher margins. Our minds would naturally go to creating an offer with a well-known designer as the brand name, a slightly older audience with more discretionary income as the target market, an exclusive channel, and expensive packaging. But this is really just a single point in space and a crowded one at that. It is a single pebble thrown in a familiar part of the pond. What if we look at the underlying dimensions of the space and stretch to the other ends to explore new places to play? What if we make up a new brand, focus on youth with very little discretionary income, use a mass retail channel, and use cheap packaging? Sound like we're fishing in the wrong place? It didn't to Unilever who created Axe to target young men with a brand positioning around virility, inexpensive plastic packaging, and adolescent fantasy advertising and sold it through mass retail. It is a premium offer providing Unilever with upsides in margins and market penetration.🌱

Opportunity storming helps us arrive at the nonobvious and counterintuitive by guiding us to explore unusual combinations of points on the dimensions. Of course, not all the ideas we develop will be successful. We don't know if some of the combinations will really work together or be an ill fit. For example, would an offer with a designer brand, a high price point, expensive materials, and mass retail work? Probably not. This is where our opportunity finders come in. The trends and insights guide us to what the ecosystem and markets are doing now and in the future, what they will prefer, and how to stretch to new benefits.

Opportunity Finders become Idea Definers

Engineering ideas to fit opportunity may at first blush feel restricting—cold, analytical, even formulaic. It is just the opposite. Opportunity landscaping gives more freedom than its alternative—which is little clear opportunity direction at all. When idea development is stimulated by a profound understanding of the space, opportunity will fuel, rather than extinguish, imagination. It allows us to navigate the opportunity space, fluently moving along the dimensions. It feeds us with new food for thought in the form of seed trends and rich insights. Unlike creativity left to its own devices, creativity guided by opportunity is more likely to be rewarded, because it is attached to a strategy the organization has bought into. Creative genius, working within opportunity, has better odds of getting its just reward, seeing its inventions and designs loved and lauded in the marketplace.

Defining opportunity
creates a hive for our ideas.
It stops our ideas from just
buzzing around and puts them
to work doing something
useful and focused. Ideas are
unpredictable alone. Some
can bring a sweet reward,
but others might sting you.

IDEA
IDEA
IDEA
IDEA
IDEA
IDEA
IDEA
IDEA

"Eurekas" don't start with people talking. They start with people thinking—

thinking in new ways and thinking **a lot.**

Brilliance in the parts

A big idea not only sits directly in the opportunity, it is also a compilation of strong ideas—like a perfectly cut diamond, each of its facets adds to its brilliance. You have to have brilliance in the parts if you are going to arrive at something stunning. So where does this individual brilliance come from?

Brilliant thinking doesn't come from "idea-kumbaya"!

Current thinking is that breakthroughs happen in groups—that brainstorming is the key to developing big ideas. But cross-functional love-ins are not the place to start if you want the stunning facets of big ideas. Brilliant ideas start with the origin of creativity itself—the creative power of the individual.

In innovation, it turns out that quality *and* quantity matter. The more ideas we have, the more likely we are to have a good one. And counter to current approaches for brainstorming, research shows that the quickest way to squash quantity is to get everyone in a group; the more people, the fewer ideas per person. This means that group ideation actually inhibits initial idea quality—something we can scarcely afford to fritter away. There are lots of reasons for the downsides of groups: social norms, a natural tendency toward convergence, thinking of what we will say next when we should be listening and considering how to solve problems. Groups also suffer from an inflated sense of success, believing that the quality of their ideas is better than it actually is, and so they quit early as they pat each other on the back for a job well done. All of these very natural tendencies mean that we produce fewer ideas and fewer quality ideas.

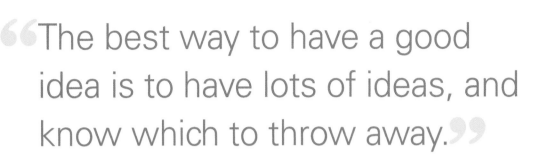

> "The best way to have a good idea is to have lots of ideas, and know which to throw away."
>
> *Linus Pauling, winner of two Nobel prizes—biochemistry and peace*

Opportunity cartography enables both the quantity and divergence we need to achieve quality ideas that we can then build into big, killer ideas. Its reach across the organization provides a tool kit that can be given to individuals in every function, stretching thinking along dimensions, challenging with insights, and confronting with impact trends. The tool kit allows people to opportunity storm by themselves to generate as many ideas as possible. When each of the business functions is creative along the lines of their deep expertise, it automatically increases the number, diversity, and quality of ideas.

This approach contradicts how many understand the domain of creativity. They see ideation as the bailiwick of the creative: the designer, the inventor, the creative agency. Such a view fails to realize that creativity is a characteristic of people, not professions. Everyone across the organization can be creative within their own realm. Tapping into the imagination of individuals, enabling them to be innovative within opportunity-rich spaces, stretching their thinking is our best bet for developing brilliant facets of big ideas.

Once people within the functions have the tools to develop ideas along the lines of their expertise, it is time to walk across the hall to work with others in the organization. The ideas will get bigger as they come in contact with new thinking, being both challenged and built upon.

Sometimes creativity is spurred by seeing a problem through the eyes of another function.

The communications team at Wrangler wanted to provide consumers with a new, highly differentiated reason to believe in their jeans. Wrangler has the top-rated jeans for comfort but needed to go beyond telling their story with football players, dogs, and trucks. In talking with R+D, they explored the physical differences between their jeans and the competition. The jeans are constructed such that they create a U shape rather than V shape where the two pant legs come together. The problem is that no consumers were aware of this. So they visualized several different ways of telling the story to one of their target markets: 25-and-older men, with a particular focus on the segment of blue-collar workers. The men were surprised and glad to understand why Wrangler jeans fit so well. Wrangler rolled out an effective commercial innovation platform in ads and in labels on the jeans that promotes a verifiable difference in their product.

Inspiration comes when we look externally.

Sherwin Williams, a global paint company, took on an environmental challenge and won industry accolades for their R+D efforts. They received recognition from the White House when they won the Presidential Green Chemistry Challenge Award for a new line of paints. The paints contain a resin they developed, which uses soybean oil and recycled plastic bottles (PET) to reduce the levels of Volatile Organic Compounds (VOCs), which can become air pollutants as the paint dries. In one year they reduced 800,000 pounds of VOCs, used 320,000 pounds of soybean oil and 250,000 pounds of PET, and eliminated 1,000 barrels of oil.

> "There is no doubt that creativity is the most important human resource of all. Without creativity, there would be no progress, and we would be forever repeating the same patterns."
>
> *Edward de Bono, author, inventor of creativity method "lateral thinking"*

Brilliant ideas happen at the seams—at the intersection between sources.

🦚 Each pair of Sources shares something in common. A good example of this is when design is informed and enabled by both expression and technology. Molson Coors leveraged this synergy by creating attention-grabbing bottles and cans for their Coors Light brand. A brand already known for cold and refreshing innovated on cold-activated packaging. When the bottle or can is at the right temperature for the ultimate consumption experience, the Rocky Mountains on the label turn blue. They accomplished this using special thermochromic inks using a leuco dye, which is colorless at warm temperatures and takes on color at cold temperatures.🦚

Sometimes a big idea is a series of brilliant ideas that together have a big impact, each requiring deep expertise and effort to implement.

🌳 PepsiCo is being lauded for global efforts in water, which they have accomplished through new organizational processes, technologies, partnerships in the ecosystem, and business models. PepsiCo's products—including Pepsi brand carbonated soft drinks, Frito-Lay snacks, Tropicana fruit juices, Quaker Oats, Gatorade, and Aquafina bottled water—all require large amounts of water to produce. Through a concerted effort, the company has achieved more than 20% improvement in global water efficiencies in a six-year period. They are implementing precision farming methods using a web-based tool "i-crop", which has increased yields and reduced water consumption in India. They have achieved a near zero-net water status at one Frito-Lay plant where 75% of the water is recycled and zero waste is sent to landfills. Beyond manufacturing, they are working to provide safe drinking water to over 1 million people through their PepsiCo Foundation. They have conserved over 16 billion liters of water, reducing both water and energy costs by as much as $45 million.

When people are motivated by a big vision such as PepsiCo's vision on water, they will generate bigger and better ideas. The momentum will increase and provide pull for even more creativity. 🌳

A single individual, a single inventor, can spark the creation of a big idea, and a single idea can become a rising star, but only when there is a good supporting cast of other ideas.

Emerging brilliance

🌳 Let's explore the brilliance of one individual and how his insight has been the starting point for what is looking like a very big idea. It started with seeing opportunity, albeit an unfortunate one. As income in developing nations has increased, people have been replacing their bicycles with cars. With this transition, accidents have skyrocketed as autos and bicycles have vied for position on the same roads. The result has been a surge in very badly broken legs. Combined with the prohibitive cost of implants and lack of trained surgeons, the trend has made for a new generation of people crippled for life.

A single doctor recognized the problem during a mission trip to Asia. Dr. Lew Zirkle invented a new implant that costs 1/1,000 of those used in developed nations. The intramedullary implant system is designed to perfectly align bones in facilities without real-time X-rays or even power systems. But he didn't stop there. Rather than trying to sell the implant, which would have failed due to the lack of trained doctors, he expanded on his idea. He developed a process for setting the bone that takes little time and, more importantly, little training. He created a training model for in-country doctors. Doing his own manufacturing has kept costs down. Finally, he created a nonprofit organization—the Surgical Implant Generation Network (SIGN) Fracture Organization—to fund training and implants. The outcome? More than 2,000 doctors in 55 countries have now treated over 100,000 patients injured not only in car crashes but also through conflicts and disasters. All of these people can now walk as a result of SIGN's work. 🌳

The individual inventor is critical for our success.

That success of inventors depends on linking, stretching, and supporting their ideas with the other Sources. Inventors have lately suffered a bad rap. They are seen as hiding away in labs and garages and not turning invention into commercialized innovation.

While it can be the case that inventors lack the ability to take their ideas to the next level, their role in innovation is critical. If we take these creative and often introverted geniuses and force them to sit in group brainstorming sessions, we will drain the brilliance and motivation from them. With a bit of cultivation and some new approaches we can have the best of both worlds. We can leverage the insights and eurekas of inventors by ensuring their ideas are shared with others who can build them into killer ideas.

Multiplying creativity

Once we have tapped the wells of creativity within ourselves and within our functions, we expand further through exploration. In this journey to big growth we may act as opportunity farmers or miners, but we should also be explorers at heart. After all, the explorers and those that followed after didn't just discover new lands; they also discovered new ways of doing things.

☕ Thomas Mayhew, who settled on what is now known as Martha's Vineyard, Massachusetts, in 1642, believed in the land rights of Indians. This belief combined with openness to their practices brought rich discoveries. The Wampanoag Indians had developed sophisticated ways of planting their three main crops—the three sisters of corn, beans, and squash—all in the same place. As the corn stalk grew, the beans would grow up the stalk, using it as a pole, and the squash would grow out around the corn and beans acting as ground cover, reducing weeds and retaining water by protecting the ground from the sun's drying heat. These methods were so successful that they have now been adopted by some organic farmers and polycroppers who use them to retain soil nutrients through biodiversity, eliminating the need for chemicals. ☕

Our opportunity landscaping has opened up the world for us, including the opportunity ecosystem with its amazing riches of insightful people. The same people who helped us discover new opportunities can now help us create bigger ideas. Producing brilliant ideas is not just a matter of creativity; it is also a matter of ongoing discovery.

At this point, our open opportunity exploration feeds our open innovation efforts.

Open innovation across the Six Sources

⚑ Open innovation can spur ideas across all six functions! During the recession when high-end fashion stores were suffering, Gucci and Ann Taylor took their suddenly empty retail spaces and leased them to up-and-coming designers. By giving these designers access to a larger customer base and by offering novel in-store experiences to their customers, they reinvigorated innovation in fashion during a time of stagnation.⚑

⚑ General Mills partnered with the Celiac Disease Foundation and leading doctors and scientists as they developed food options for people affected by the ailment. Celiac disease is an autoimmune disorder that damages the small intestine when foods with gluten—a protein in wheat, rye, and barley—are consumed. While the disease affects about 1% of the population, entire households of people impacted often go gluten-free, as does a growing segment concerned about gluten's impact on health in general. With input from the outside, General Mills developed products for a market segment that struggled to find good alternatives to wheat products. They reformulated cereals such as Rice Chex and created the first mainstream gluten-free products—Betty Crocker baking mixes for cookies, cakes, and brownies. They helped to launch GlutenFreely.com, devoted to selling a range of brands and foods. With over 300 products labeled gluten-free, they are creating a big idea that is getting bigger with the help of others.⚑

When we co-create with the ecosystem, there is no end to the potential impacts. Ideas get even bigger with openness across all Six Sources.

⚑ This is certainly what Eastman Chemical Company discovered. Eastman, which was spun off from Kodak, makes a wide range of plastics and chemicals. One of its legacy materials is cellulose ester—the stuff that camera film is made of and a plastic that is made from wood. As film sales decreased, Eastman had a challenge—how to create new variants and discover new applications. They went out to the ecosystem and talked to scientists, engineers, designers, universities, and consumer goods companies. The collaborations resulted in many new applications, but by far the most interesting outcome came from interactions with designers. Designers identified a big unmet need, but it wasn't for a new material. It was to better understand the materials in Eastman's portfolio. Designers influence the materials chosen by consumer goods companies for a wide variety of products but don't often have the science backgrounds needed to understand the properties of new materials. So they end up sticking with materials they used while in school. By collaborating with designers, Eastman developed new physical communication tools that designers could feel and touch and that demonstrated the properties of the materials. Eastman further developed a network of designers and engaged them through design forums and a website to induce them to talk to each other about materials. This snowballed into designers discovering even more new uses. For example, one firm discovered that the wood-based plastic had interesting sound properties. They created an award-winning guitar that landed Eastman's materials on the cover of *BusinessWeek*.

The bigger win was that Eastman, with a new design focus, was able to work directly with the consumer goods companies who were several steps away from them in the value chain. The strategy and resulting Eastman Innovation Lab won top industry awards, became the gold standard for materials marketing, and created such momentum within Eastman that it has affected both the innovation culture and the bottom line.⚑

Open innovation beckons to every function, to every individual to be more open.

Brewing bigger ideas

With treasure troves of ideas, we now explore how to combine them in ways that create winning offers. After all, our consumers buy the whole product not the parts. They don't have the luxury of buying a brand separate from a product, a product separate from a price, or a package from one company and the contents from another. The whole offer is what the consumer takes home in their shopping bag. Products end up being Six-Sourced, even if we aren't building them that way! We need to come together to form big ideas where the parts all work together to tell the same story, the same value proposition.

Truly big ideas are those where the parts aren't just piled on top of each other. They are put together so that they interact with each other to become something new. Creating big ideas is not a process of hammering out offers that are a compilation of individual pieces. Instead, it is more like a great brewing process—the interaction of the very best ingredients, in the right combination, at a specific temperature, over a critical time period, leading to the perfect brew. A big idea brewing process allows for nuance, influence, and accents to develop as the ingredients interact.

We can get a jump on driving interactions between elements of an offer when we interact among ourselves. Who better to see and form relationships between the Six Sources than people from the six functions? Cross-functionality, by its nature, brings together people with different skills, experiences, viewpoints, responsibilities, and resources. While there was a time for us to work quietly by ourselves, it is now time to come together to create something much bigger than we could create on our own. Add to our ranks some external ecosystem members to help the blending process and give the emerging ideas a sniff test, throw in some consumers to quickly give feedback, and you have the best of all worlds to brew and test big ideas. It is at this point that we not only create ideas, we also kill ideas! Kill ideas that have wandered outside the opportunities we have selected, and kill ideas that will underdeliver on the opportunity. **Killing ideas of an inferior nature so that we can create killer ideas— killer ideas that create big yields.**

The North Face did this through a process called a rapid brewery. They joined with an outside technology company who had a new fiber component, and brought in a cross-functional team from both companies. They engaged designers and innovation experts, their ad agency, editors of sports sections, a renowned mountain climber, and bloggers. All these people came together to examine the individual parts of an idea for a new clothing line for athletes— the clothing, branding, price points, go-to-market plan, and positioning. They tested the elements with early adopters from the athletic community to see which was strongest. They then brought the pieces together into idea bundles and tested multidimensional offers with a new group of athletes. The result was the launch of a successful range of clothing using FlashDry, a material innovation that rapidly removes moisture through multiple layers of clothing to keep the athlete out and active longer. The approach turned open innovation into a market success.

Big ideas don't come from Bob the Builder! They come from Bob the Brewer!

Big ideas emerge when we tap into both the best of individuals and the best of teams.

Cultivation

We have chosen the right soil with our opportunity landscaping. We are engineering ideas to fit the opportunity with opportunity storming and grafting them together through cross-functional processes such as the rapid brewery. But we are lacking one more element of precision farming—that of cultivating the plant. Even big ideas need a little extra love and attention.

New ideas can be cultivated in much the same way as new seed strains. It takes time, with many tests and tweaks in petri dishes, then in hothouses, and eventually into the fields.

We test these precious engineered ideas differently than the way we may have tested ideas in the past. Most ideas are tested in their parts rather than as a whole. Food companies perform taste tests independent of online tests of brand concepts. Industrial companies survey customers about individual product features out of context of the total product and service offering. Presenting people with the whole offer, rather than individual parts, is critical to get a sense of what will happen once launched.

The bigger the idea, the smaller the test!

Testing killer ideas can start with mini launches to our own staff, a beta test with a single customer, or small test markets in a closed environment such as a university or a city. These tests are as much to convince the internal organization that there is potential as they are to gather needed feedback!

🌳 When a team at M&M's came up with the idea of personalizing the candies with consumers' names or messages for special events, they met with concerns that it was too small an idea. The first foray was to print the candies for a special event within the company. A big hit, they soon received requests from across the company for other events. This led the team to find an ink-jet approach to printing, which reduced set-up costs to zero. Soon they launched it to staff for personalized messages—a launch designed to test price and order-size sensitivity. After only four hours they had enough demand to keep them busy for a month. The team doubled the price, turned on the website again and sold out in two hours. Despite the demand, there were internal fears it wasn't sustainable. A consumer research study was commissioned that revealed even more demand and led to further raising the price and reducing minimum order sizes.

Despite internal resistance from a company built on selling tons, the business was eventually launched as My M&M's. They have added new features such as the ability to print jpegs on the candies. Cultivating this idea, from putting toes in the water to jumping in, led to higher margins and the launch of an idea that was seen as risky. 🌳

Innovate for choosing, not just using!

As we seed opportunity, we have to select the right ideas that will produce a big yield, and therefore we must be prepared to let others go. No organization has an unlimited budget for growth. Invariably we have to make some tough choices and select which ideas to kill and which to grow. Rather like growing vegetables, young seedlings must be thinned to leave room for the strongest to grow. Thinning our portfolio gives us more resources and attention for the healthy offers.

Cultivating our seedlings also requires managing the environment. Killer ideas are ideas with advocates. The ecosystem will ultimately kiss or kill our offers. So let's get them on our side early. When they participate with us in brewing big ideas, they are more likely to toast the outcomes.

Sometimes convincing the external ecosystem to advocate for us is easier than getting that same support from our organization. Our own colleagues can prove to be bigger detractors than the market! We get around this in part through our cross-functional efforts. Ideas generated cross-functionally will be more likely to build broad support and address concerns early. But beware, if the ideas are really big they will also amass detractors ready to fight to exhaustion. We shouldn't fear this conflict, but instead embrace it as a good sign that we are on the right track. If the ideas were safe or close in, we wouldn't have opposition. There would be nothing to object to. A killer idea will be polarizing, because it is different from what has been done in the past, which is exactly what we want when pursuing big growth.

A final component of cultivation is timing. As we develop ideas we must not forget that opportunity comes from change, so it's on the move. Farmers have a critical window of time to plant crops, waiting for the last frost but not delaying too long. Some ideas are planted too early before the soil of the market and the broader ecosystem has adequately warmed up to them. Alternatively, other ideas are launched too late. Whether it's fear of failure or convolutions of workplace democracy, we run the risk of making no decision or delaying action while the opportunity glides by.

> "Farming looks mighty easy when your plow is a pencil, and you're a thousand miles from the cornfield."
>
> *Dwight D. Eisenhower, former U.S. president*

OPPORTUNITY THINKING

Opportunity-derived ideas are bigger; they kill off ideas that don't fit and become killer ideas in the market.

The Six Sources of Opportunity are also the Six Sources of Big Ideas.

Grafting together big ideas requires brilliance from both the individual and the organization.

Our Opportunity Finders are Idea Definers, providing guidance and stimulation for creativity.

BIG
MINING

While the Spanish were down south chasing gold and silver, the French were up north chasing beavers. Their passion for the furry creatures came from fashion—the pelts could be turned into the felt used in hats. Beavers were becoming few and far between in Russia so the French had an open market in Europe, where a growing population meant there were more heads needing stylish hats. The business of beavers took the French far and wide. They traveled up the St. Lawrence River, through the Great Lakes, along the Hudson, and eventually down the Mississippi all the way to the Gulf of Mexico. Their close relationship with the First Nations Indians, and later the Huron and Ottawa—living side by side, learning customs and language, and working in partnership —expanded opportunity. Together they explored, trapped, and traveled. Besides netting some good income from pelts, their efforts in beaver trapping resulted in the single largest exploration of North America, its geography, and resources.

The French mined the beaver population—almost to extinction. They did so through a series of business and market-building efforts that included establishing a trading center in what is now Quebec, developing long-lasting relationships with the indigenous nations, learning how to brave the cold, bitter winters, and continually exploring the land for more beaver colonies.

Mining opportunity requires similar diligence and persistence. Eventually farming of opportunities will and should give way to opportunity mining. Miners dig deeper, shoring up the internal structures, refreshing the brands, extending the product ranges, expanding distribution, and reducing costs to reach new markets.

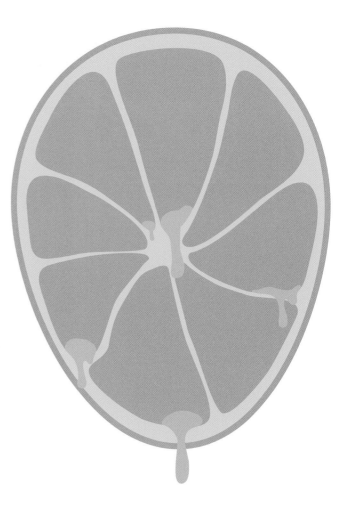

Mining means we make the most of the opportunity we have identified and invested in. It means capturing every last drop of value.

Barrick Gold Corporation, a Canadian company, has built a business model around getting every ounce of gold possible from a property. Now, that might sound like an obvious thing to do until you realize that there aren't big gold nuggets sitting around. The gold is in the form of microscopic, atomic-sized particles. It is embedded in different kinds of rock and requires all-new methods of extraction. Barrick figured out many of the latest technologies for discovery and extraction. Imagine being a small company in the 1980s and buying a new property, the Goldstrike property in Nevada, where you have estimated that there are 600,000 ounces of gold embedded deep in the rock. It sounds promising, albeit a bit daunting to get to. But Barrick didn't stop there. Their science, technology, and partnerships with suppliers allowed them to mine a stunning 40 million ounces, and they now can verify that there are 12 million more ounces out there. The gold near the surface was processed with simple solution chemistry. Deeper ore required innovating high temperature roasting processes to extract the gold. Cash flows from Goldstrike, which were substantial, allowed Barrick to buy other companies and properties where they use their same methods to get the most from the property. They are now the number one gold producer in the world. And they have managed to do all this while achieving recognition for their sustainability track record. They are listed on the Dow Jones Sustainability World Index and are one of the top 100 companies globally for sustainability.

Mining for gold isn't all that different from mining an opportunity. The value close to the surface—what is obvious and easy to estimate at the start—is easily captured. Early adopters are often in the obvious markets. But to get at the deeper value we have to find new methods of extraction. We will have to innovate across the other Six Sources. New distribution channels, features, designs, business models, and spokespeople will be needed to persuade the later adopters. We will look for even more imaginative ways to leap from one market segment to another or add features that create entirely new value propositions. The point is that opportunity mining is going to require creativity, new insights, and good ideas just like opportunity farming.

As if mining gold, we need to be thinking ahead about how we mine our markets sustainably.

Sustainable mining

Sustainable mining practice is not an oxymoron! The top mining companies, such as Barrick, are starting projects with planning for land reclamation—strategizing to minimize disturbance of the environment, erosion of soil, and pollution of the water sources. The goal of reclamation is to quickly return the land that has been mined to productive use. Shining examples of innovation have resulted in Florida phosphate mines being transformed into golf courses and land in California rapidly being returned to farming of everything from hay to tomatoes, grapes to strawberries.

We, too, need to find ways to mine our opportunity landscapes sustainably. **Applying sustainable practices in opportunity mining means we don't damage the opportunity through erosion.**

Opportunity erosion happens when we erode trust through inferior quality, dangerous products, unethical employment practices, and false sustainability claims that undermine our brand equity. We erode margins by commoditizing products and neglecting to innovate. Our competitive advantage from know-how erodes when we fail to guard our trade secrets or retain employees so knowledge doesn't walk out the door. We erode the natural resources we rely on by not employing sustainable practices. Opportunity mining requires creative approaches to sustain value and keep the market in a healthy condition so that it will be open to opportunity farming when the time is right.

🍄 BP, formerly British Petroleum, was seen as eroding trust through greenwashing. In its campaign "Beyond Petroleum," the company claimed that they were diversifying their energy portfolio with renewables when in fact only a fraction of their assets were not in oil. Trust eroded further with the Deepwater Horizon disaster in the Gulf of Mexico. But it wasn't just trust of BP that was damaged; the leakage spilled over to other oil companies who were endeavoring to achieve both safety and sustainability.

Wal-Mart has innovated relentlessly in driving down costs and has brought much efficiency to the world of retailing. But they also are seen as having eroded markets. Their presence has spelled the demise of smaller retailers in communities, causing the notion of local business to all but dry up across rural America. The loss of jobs has eroded the customer base Wal-Mart itself relies on.🍄

Opportunity mining requires the same creativity and discovery processes as opportunity farming. This innovation close in—refreshing brands, rationalizing product lines, and improving features—can be more challenging than innovating far from the core. It requires a disciplined approach to creativity, supported through opportunity cartography, which sets tight guardrails for where opportunity lies. Mining means keeping the offer fresh—one source at a time in some cases. It might involve adding an attribute that is on trend, improving the design of a package, openly innovating on new manufacturing processes with a smaller carbon footprint, or connecting through an innovative ad campaign. Opportunity mining requires the same elements of creativity and discovery and the same disciplines around understanding opportunity.

We mine opportunities when we tap more deeply into a *market need* and provide ever better solutions.

Kimberly-Clark's effort in capturing the full opportunity for facial tissues is, well, nothing to sneeze at! You may not realize all the science that goes into something you are so quick to toss away! Kleenex brand Cool Touch tissues have sophisticated phase change materials in them so that they feel cool to the touch for a suffering nose. Anti-Viral tissues have a moisture-activated middle layer that kills 99.9% of cold and flu viruses. A new Sneeze Shield tissue keeps moisture from getting through to fingers so that fewer germs are spread. Kimberly-Clark has a larger vision around germ control that has resulted in a partnership with the Centers for Disease Control in the United States, focusing on a hand hygiene effort. The approach Kimberly-Clark has taken has turned their tissue brand into a killer idea, a constellation of ideas that blend efforts across many of the Six Sources bringing killer returns while their products are busy killing germs.

The pattern of innovations in tissues is consistent with Kimberly-Clark's overall strategy of investing in insight on consumer needs and science to continually improve the benefits of their products. They have done this in every one of their categories. Watching parents with babies has sparked innovations in Huggies diapers, leading them to expand into new ages with Huggies Pull-Ups, new parts of the day with Good Nites, and new occasions with Little Swimmers. Kimberly-Clark has a track record of mining opportunity by finding new needs to meet and new ways to meet them.

Sometimes we achieve growth by mining our *technologies* more deeply.

Milliken, a global performance materials, chemicals, and textile company, is mining new opportunities from existing technology platforms by looking at new problems to be solved. Their capabilities led them to design fabric technologies for active sportswear—including technologies that allow materials to wick moisture away from the skin. Having licensed that technology to clothing brands, they sought other ways to leverage their intellectual property. The big Aha came as they realized that the same properties that make their fabrics comfortable for athletes would lend themselves to the healing of wounds. Chronic wounds such as those of people with diabetes require constant movement of moisture away from the body. Milliken discovered that their know-how in both textiles and chemistry could do the trick while giving patients the same cool, dry feeling athletes seek. They created a small start-up business within the corporation that is delivering their technologies in the form of dressings that are now healing the most stubborn of wounds.

Milliken's company history is one of going deep and developing new ways to extract more value from opportunities. They have taken their industrial textiles, which are used in duct tape and roofing, and worked closely with a company out of the UK that first developed concrete cloth. It's an amazing invention that can be rolled out and watered, and it magically takes form. They leverage their technology portfolio and design expertise to maximize their potential while adding elements of new partners or markets to capture the value of opportunities more completely.

Sometimes we mine an opportunity with a focus on a single problem.

In the case of Timken, that problem is friction. Timken was started in 1898 by Henry Timken when he invented the tapered roller bearing, an invention designed to reduce friction and wear in carriages. Friction may sound like a fact of life—the nature of things mechanical—but that is not how Timken sees it. They are reducing friction and increasing energy efficiency in every way imaginable. They have developed new designs for their bearings that actually improve lubrication effectiveness and give the bearings longer life. They were the first movers in developing thin film coatings for use on critical surfaces to make their products more wear-resistant than previously possible. They have advanced surface measurement and modeling techniques in their industry, moving from a 2-D to 3-D perspective via new-to-the-world algorithms. Ongoing efforts in bearing design and performance modeling have advanced their ability to design and diagnose both well-known and new mechanical systems. They are on the leading edge of the science of tribology—the study of interacting surfaces in relative motion—which has led them to a better understanding and being able to predict the role of debris contamination in system life, allowing them to serve any industry where there is motion! Timken's bearings are in the landing gear of airplanes that accelerate from 0 to 2,000 rpm in a fraction of a second. They have enabled exploration of Mars because their products work in extreme conditions. Timken's focus on friction and motion has taken their science and products to places far from where they started.

One company is mining a consumer need, another is mining technology platforms, while the third is mining a problem. Of course, each company has also expanded beyond these areas, investing in new spaces. But of interest here is the diligence and conscientiousness they have shown in mining their core opportunities. They have extracted more value through continuous improvement and innovation as evidenced by the thousands of patents held by each—a number that is growing year after year.

Of equal importance, they are mining sustainably. Kimberly-Clark is regularly at the top of the list for consumer products on the Dow Jones Sustainability World Index. The Milliken family of companies has been certified carbon negative due to the 130,000 acres of forests they manage and their continuous improvements in manufacturing. Timken is also working to improve efficiency and reduce energy use in every mechanical industry including, most recently, wind power. The results of all these efforts have been truly impressive, with sustainable and maintainable growth. All three companies have been in business since the late 1800s, and each has grown significantly. Kimberly-Clark has over $20 billion in revenue and employs over 56,000 people. Milliken is one of the largest privately held companies in the world and has over 7,000 employees. Timken has over 21,000 employees and $5 billion in revenue.

Companies that know how to mine sustainably, creating value for customers while not eroding the opportunities, often share another characteristic. They are highly ethical. Their ethics translate into culture and practices that are fair to their customers, competitors, employees, and stakeholders—a balancing act that requires deeply held values often going back to their founders. All three companies have received the highest levels of recognition, being named year after year on the list of the top 100 companies in the world by Ethisphere.

Opportunity mining clearly requires big ideas to keep the market fresh and extend product lines. It also requires the mind-set of the explorer—to have eyes to the horizon to see what might be coming. And it requires that we think a bit like the farmer who is always on the lookout for better ways to cultivate.

The guardians of our brands and businesses are not relegated to business as usual, but should continually have an eye out for business as *unusual*.

From mining to farming and back again

Opportunities change! What might have been an opportunity for mining may become ripe for farming as our consumers evolve. So how do we know when to modify our approach? No one wants to continually develop new offers when the old ones haven't captured the value they can. On the other hand, we don't want to be caught unaware by a competitor introducing a new offer. The answer is found in exploration: The organization that is continually scanning the environment for what is new will sense the winds of change on the horizon. The same exploration tools we used to discover opportunity are what we need to discover how opportunity might be evolving. The same exploration tools that help us get to brilliant ideas through openness to the ecosystem are what we will need to snap up new ideas—new ideas with which we might even obsolete ourselves!

Our approach to pursuing both opportunities and ideas must have us acting in three roles— that of explorer, farmer, and miner. When we do this, we not only create big ideas and keep our ideas fresh, we also turn around and create new opportunity. Perhaps the most exciting thing about cultivating really killer ideas is that they don't just produce revenue; they also spark new opportunity. They awaken needs that lay unarticulated, create new experiences, and change cultures. If we have an explorer's curiosity, the empathy of the farmer to learn the land and cultivate the seeds, and the intuition and diligence of the miner to follow the value and extract the maximum possible, we will create growth that is truly sustainable.

🌳 The story of Tupperware is worth understanding as, while it is an old one, it is a story of big growth from a combination of exploration, farming, and mining, and it is a story of how a killer idea created even more opportunity and eventually changed a culture. Mr. Tupper took advantage of the invention of plastics to develop

his famous containers for holding foods—bowls with lids that sealed tightly. He came up with a clever brand expression that challenged consumers to "burp" their container to create a better seal. One day, he noticed that his largest customer was not a department store but an individual. Brownie Wise was a single mother who was buying up large quantities of these containers and selling them through parties. He reached out to her, and in 1951 the two joined forces, combining Mr. Tupper's innovation on technology and design with Ms. Wise's innovation in business model, organization, and market.

The outcome was a killer idea. The direct marketing approach of home parties was born. It accelerated growth at Tupperware—sales multiplied by 25 times in just three years even with the gutsy decision to pull the product from department store shelves. The impact of this new sales model rippled through the very culture. Women began selling Tupperware in their homes under the radar of husbands who disapproved of women working. The new income led to independence, funds to get an education, and ultimately changed views of women working. While Ivy League women's schools such as Smith College and Vassar ushered in a new era of independence among the elite, something as simple as selling plastic bowls through parties was giving a broader range of women new views of what was possible.

The opportunity didn't stay put though. It expanded worldwide, and now a whole host of other companies are using the party method or other derivatives of Ms. Wise's approaches. Today, Tupperware has over 2.6 million salespeople worldwide and sales of over $3 billion. The sales methods are used to sell products from nutritional supplements to children's toys. The largest of direct sales companies is global cosmetic company Avon, with sales of over $11 billion and a staggering 6.5 million salespeople. Tupperware's beginnings have influenced women worldwide through companies such as Brazil's Natura cosmetics with sales of over $3 billion and 1.4 million salespeople; Germany's maker of appliances and JAFRA cosmetics, Vorwerk & Co, with sales over $3 billion and over 600,000 salespeople; and Luxembourg's Oriflame beauty products with sales over $2 billion and 3.6 million salespeople.

The opportunity is shifting and changing further. Women aren't the only ones knocking on doors. Men are selling everything from lawn care equipment to automobile products. Perhaps the most fun is ManCave Worldwide. They have MEATings—which are guy parties where the host hangs out at their barbeque, teaching the latest in grilling and smoking meats, all the time selling a range of tools, meats, and spices.

The Tupperware story shows us that exploring while mining can lead to new farming of opportunities, taking smaller ideas and making them bigger, and even creating new opportunity for ourselves and others.

Killer ideas allow us to both capture opportunity today and be the authors of opportunity in the future.

The principle of exploring, mining, and farming all at the same time applies not only to business now but business in the past.

⚓ Returning to where this story of big ideas started, we find that the countries that sent explorers, miners, and farmers out together benefited with finds of new ore and new crops. But the story takes an interesting turn. Spain, one of the earliest sponsors of exploration, was also one of the first to bring back silver, gold, and the food of the gods, chocolate. But they did not invest as heavily in cultivating new crops as did the English. They pursued mining over farming. Their lack of cultivation of newly discovered crops resulted in trade imbalances, as all their gold and silver went to countries with the resources they needed to buy. The countries that explored, mined, and farmed were the ones that won in the new economy. England was so successful that eventually the sun never set on the British Empire. ⚓

🌱 Nintendo provides us with an excellent example of exploring, farming, and mining an opportunity. In 1898 they began as a playing card company. Their passion for games led them, many years later in 1974, to enter the emerging video game space. They started small—just distributing Magnavox's video game console for televisions. But a year later, they entered the arcade game market, and then after two years they started to make their own Color TV Game consoles.

You might have played the game that, in 1981, first put their name on the map—Donkey Kong. They generated significant revenue and profits from licensing the big gorilla to other systems. But then things got even better with a plumber in a hat who said "Itsa me, Mario!" In 1985 they launched Super Mario Brothers, one of the best-selling games of all time.

While they were mining the game development side of the opportunity, they turned their attention to handheld games. They launched the Game Boy handheld system in 1989, followed by versions for the pocket and in color. They essentially obsoleted themselves with their development of the Nintendo DS, followed later by the 3DS.

Their battle for dominance in consoles has waxed and waned with introductions including the Nintendo 64 in 1996 and the GameCube in 2001, and then, with advances in motion sensors and touch screens, they introduced the Nintendo Wii and WiiU.

Gaming is a big opportunity, and Nintendo has attacked it from all sides—hardware and software, at home and at the arcade. Unlike console companies Sony and Microsoft, Nintendo develops its own games. They have farmed new spaces and mined them, once established. But perhaps most interesting in recent history is the new value they have tapped into with the Wii. The Wii finally penetrated two segments that lagged in adoption—women and an older demographic. Their combination of hardware and games has enabled the Wii to unlock new value in the opportunity that had been waiting there all along. More than 80% of female gamers use the Wii as compared to 40% of male gamers. In addition, the Wii Fit has opened up new usage occasions by tapping into exercise time.

Any way you look at it, Nintendo has successfully expanded opportunity. They have repeatedly explored new areas, new technologies, and new or unmet consumer needs within the ever-changing territory. Their explorations have led to farming new spaces, planting new-to-the-world offers, and mining the areas where they were having success.🌳

Bringing together opportunity mining, farming, and exploration are keys to our growth. With opportunities on the move, we really have no choice in the matter. In fact, this is how we achieve sustainable growth: by recognizing that opportunities change and we must change with them; recognizing that every opportunity, in its lifetime, will require both an evolutionary, mining-intensive approach and a revolutionary, farming-intensive approach. While opportunity exploration reveals when the tipping point between the two is near, it is killer ideas that might actually tip the balance. Killer ideas can move us from mining back to farming, from evolution back to revolution, and from idea back to opportunity as they create a wake of opportunity behind them.

The secret to this agile approach is tricky.

Love the opportunity more than the idea.

When you love the opportunity more than the idea—more than the brand, the technology, or the resulting product—you will keep your eyes on the opportunity and all its nuances. You will always be on the lookout for better ways to meet needs, new customers to serve, new places to distribute, and new ways to monetize the value. You will be passionate about getting the most from the opportunity and giving the most to it. By loving opportunities more than our ideas, we are free to follow the ore, free to till new ground, and free to explore new lands when the time is right.

Free to create killer ideas!

OPPORTUNITY THINKING

Mining opportunity invites us to dig deep and to creatively capture all the potential.

Sustainable mining retains the health of the opportunity.

Opportunity is on the move and requires us to be explorers, farmers, and miners.

CHAPTER 7

BIG FUTURE

Columbus to Cabot, Vasco da Gama to Vasquez, Sir Francis Drake to Sir Walter Raleigh . . .

⚓ All these famed explorers set their sights on distant lands and their minds on ships, maps, crews, and supplies. Little did they know their expeditions were sparking a revolution in Europe. Not a political revolution—a commercial revolution. Exploring new lands required new forms of business—new ways to share risk, insure expeditions, and exchange goods. It was the birth of many business systems we take for granted today. An opportunity in and of itself, intertwined with all the other opportunities of the day. The one could not have been realized without the other. ⚓

Opportunity begets opportunity.

While we recognize the who's who of explorers, the real *who* of growth during that period extends well beyond those who set sail. Countless people both paved the way for expeditions and shaped opportunity in the aftermath. The opportunity ecosystem was rich with participants, each taking on critical roles, each contributing in their own ways.

Opportunity requires a village, a vanguard, and then some!

Opportunity requires visionaries to see ahead, gather the resources, and draw others in.

Visionaries

⚓ Well before the notion to sail entered the minds of Christopher (Columbus), Ferdinand (Magellan), or Hernan (Cortes) there was Henry! Prince Henry the Navigator of Portugal (1394–1460) was a visionary who dreamed of a passage to India around the tip of Africa, years before the Turks blocked the land route. He led development of a faster ship, the caravel, two of which were used by Columbus. He studied seas, tides, and stars and fostered advancements in cartography and sailing. He built an R+D center and university all in one—the Institute at Sagres. The institute included libraries, an astronomical observatory, shipbuilding facilities, a chapel, and housing for staff. ⚓

Government and nongovernment agencies

⚓ Businesses alone weren't big enough to fund all the expeditions or the arts and sciences of the Renaissance. It was kicked off by government. Government endeavors spurred opportunity for many and, equally, disaster for others—in distant lands. After years of being the patron of individual inventors, one government created an open innovation model, akin to the first X Prize.

The X Prize of today was established by the nonprofit X Prize Foundation to accelerate innovation in categories such as energy and education. They are best known for their $10 million prize in 2007 for personal space travel. It propelled the personal space industry into being, just about 38 years after we put a man on the moon. In 1676 the British Parliament declared navigation the greatest scientific problem of the age, and 38 years later in 1714 they offered their first X Prize—a substantial financial prize for creating devices to measure longitude. The results were the marine chronometer, the lunar distance methodology, and the octant. ⚓

Opportunity requires funders willing to invest in what does not yet exist!

Scientists and scholars

⚓ Before the results of the navigation X Prize, calculating longitude was a bit of a challenge. If you could just figure out the time of day where you were at sea and the time back at port, you would have a rough idea of your longitude. But how could you do that when it wasn't a function of how long you had been at sea? Your best bet was to depend on the work of Abraham Zacuto, who published tables of star movements to help. The tables, the Epherimides, were so valuable they were used for over 200 years. When Columbus was trying to return home from his fourth voyage, the locals weren't of a mind to help him build a ship for the journey. He noticed that Zacuto's tables predicted an upcoming lunar eclipse. Warning that he would banish the moon if they didn't help out, he soon gained their respect and some extra provisions when the eclipse arrived right on schedule. ⚓

Opportunities require scientists and scholars
to stretch the potential through invention.

Business leaders

⛴ With the arrival of gold and silver came advances in currency and finally a consistent value for the coin. This spurred greater distribution of wealth and more eager investors. By 1553 if you happened to have a bit of money you might invest in the newly established Company of Merchant Adventurers to New Lands—one of the first companies to offer joint stock in expeditions. The notion of owning stock was taken up a notch when the Dutch East India Company created the first stock exchange—the Amsterdam Stock Exchange—which allowed investors to buy and sell shares as they wished. Of course, investing in voyages was still pretty risky, which meant someone needed to figure out how to insure trips. The solution came from an unlikely place—a humble coffee shop that published a newspaper with the latest updates on voyages. The news helped the independent insurers, who sipped their coffee, to better assess risk. The owner of the shop soon decided to get a piece of the action and established what would be the longest-standing insurance company. His name? Henry Lloyd. His coffee shop? Lloyd's of London. ⛴

Opportunity requires both risk takers and those who reduce risk, those who *ensure* returns and those who *insure* returns.

Business organization

As companies grew so did the way they organized themselves. One of the trickier aspects of exploration was provisioning; preserving food on ships was no easy task. Cargo holds were filled with what wouldn't spoil—dried lentils, honey, olives, salted fish, and beer and wine. What they weren't full of was fruit and vegetables, and that led to scurvy, which killed over 1 million sailors from 1500 to 1800. The Dutch East India Company addressed this problem in 1652 by setting up a permanent colony on the Cape of Good Hope in order to provide fresh fruit, meat, water, and other goods for ships on their way east. The reduced deaths made sailing a much more appealing profession!

Opportunities live to see another day when people innovate around how to capture them.

The market

⚓ Explorations awoke another revolution—a revolution in flavor, food, and agriculture. Farmers, shops, restaurants, chefs, and consumers all opened their minds and palates to new experiences, creating demand for new goods. More than just spices, the movement of goods from one place to another radically changed what was grown and eaten. In fact, entire food cultures and national identities were molded as a result. Just imagine, before the time of Columbus, there were neither tomatoes in Italy nor chocolate in Switzerland. The Irish didn't know what a potato was nor had the Hungarians become famous for paprika. Equally there weren't chili peppers in Thailand nor tea in China. Florida had no oranges, Colombia had no coffee, Ecuador had no bananas, and Hawaii no pineapples.

Worldwide, opportunity from farm to fork was altered. Change in one place produced change in another as resources were shifted from one location to another. Consumers and retailers all joined in the melee of opportunity creation, both consuming and innovating in new ways. ⚓

Opportunity becomes a feeding frenzy when people join in its creation.

Opportunity ecosystem

There are countless stories of people who saw opportunity and took hold of it. The ecosystem was brimming with creative, ambitious people who took advantage of the changes afoot—but there were plenty who opted out. Plenty who didn't hear opportunity knocking, didn't look for it on the horizon, or didn't dig deep to do something creative.

Why did some take chances, risk failure, disappointment, and fortune on the unknown, while others around them were content to do things as they had done in the past? What motivated these few?

An appetite for growth

The appetites and motivations varied. For some it was to satisfy their physical appetites and taste buds with a nouveau cuisine. For others it was an appetite for knowledge—scholars and scientists satisfying their curiosity. For many it was personal drive to see what they could accomplish, while others thirsted for adventure. And for some it was an appetite for money and power. Both the bright and dark sides of hungering for growth had people pursuing opportunity. These were the people whose eyes were open, always on the lookout for opportunity. But, unbeknownst to many of them, they weren't just taking advantage of opportunity, they were also creating it. Their endeavors to discover and produce new value and ways of doing business expanded and shaped opportunity for themselves and others.

In hindsight, it is easy to see the opportunity that surrounded them. It is easy to look back, label these periods of innovation with terms like Age of Exploration or Commercial Revolution, and imagine how exciting they must have been. But the advances recorded took hundreds of years, with plenty of economic ups and downs along the way, and it is doubtful that everyone was aware of or shared in the excitement of the time.

"Opportunities always look bigger *going* than coming."

Mark Twain, author

We live in an equally exciting time with advances in information, biology, electronics, energy, materials, globalization, sustainable resources, life expectancy, standard of living, and more. Our world, as theirs, is getting smaller, more connected, faster, and tastier. We live in as rich and varied an opportunity ecosystem as they did, and also have potential to see, spark, and stretch opportunity, assuming that we look for its potential.

Think back to the koi example. We said the koi was an idea and the pond was the opportunity. If you want a big fish, you need a big pond. If you want a big idea, you need a big opportunity.

But aren't we also like the koi? While the koi is said to moderate its actual growth by its sense of the dimension of the pond, don't we also moderate our growth efforts based on our view of potential, both as individuals and as organizations? We try harder when we have hope for a brighter future—hope that stems from our view of opportunity. We go after big growth when we see ourselves in the center of a big pond—a big opportunity. That is where our efforts and ideas have room to grow, but we ourselves have room to grow, too—grow in our capabilities, in new experiences, in accomplishments, wealth, stature, character, the good we can create, and our legacies.

There can't be much growth for us if our pond is small, has no room for expansion, and we're stuck swimming with the same fish. We might enjoy, for a time, becoming the big fish in a little pond, but the prospects for growth will remain limited without change. The change that is needed is to find a bigger pond. Or perhaps, just maybe, the change we really need is to better understand the dimensions of the pond we are in. It is true that we might be swimming in a small pond and need some new scenery. It is also possible, though, that we've simply failed to see how big a pond it is, just like many people have. **We may be swimming in a big opportunity and not even know it.**

Our growth will be moderated by what we believe of our opportunities.

The key to a bright future of growth, of whatever kind we desire, is to see our world as opportunity rich. This is the crux of Opportunity Thinking. Opportunity Thinking gives us new ways to see opportunity.

It takes our thinking from ideas to opportunities. It expands our efforts from one Source to Six. It translates the Six Sources of opportunity into Six Sources of Big Growth. It gives us tools for exploration as well as ways to use what we find to graft together Killer Ideas.

Opportunity Thinking helps us see the truth about opportunity itself—namely that there is a lot more than we realize. It bursts forth from change, lays hidden in unstretched dimensions, whispers to us from new insights. It sits next to us on a plane, walks by us in the hallway, and rings us on the phone. It comes to mind in the shower, while on a jog, or in the lab. It is waiting to be discovered and created as we ourselves discover and create.

The world is truly rich with opportunity—if we will only open our eyes and ears. Not that we become Opportunity Pollyannas, wearing rose-colored glasses, believing that everything we see is an opportunity. Just the opposite. Opportunity Thinking is about being realistic. Both the optimist and pessimist miss true opportunity. Optimists see it everywhere, deluding themselves into thinking markets always want what they have, their capabilities will satisfy any need, and the check is always in the mail. They live in a world of perpetual tailwinds. Pessimists see just the opposite. Their funding is never enough, capabilities inadequate or underappreciated, and their markets are always looking the other way. They live in a world of perpetual headwinds.

Opportunity Thinking drives a new realism for growth that is independent of our predispositions and personalities. It gives us a more disciplined view of opportunity—one that recognizes both its complexities and abundance.

Opportunity Thinking provides us with an informed view of opportunity itself.

We begin to understand that potential exists at all times, by definition, because it is fostered by things inherent in this world—a steady stream of unmet needs and wants in markets, the inventiveness and creativity innate in people, and an environment that is always changing, always shuffling the deck, creating new conditions to foster opportunity where it previously wasn't.

If we know what to listen for, opportunity will constantly call to us. But when opportunity harkens to us, we will generally only act if we hear its call in every part of our being. Pursuing opportunity—pursuing growth—requires more than head knowledge. It requires heart knowledge. After all, it is risky business. The explorers of old braved pirates, poison arrows, shipwreck, mutinies, and deprivation. Journeys expected to take weeks, took months. To venture out and take hold of opportunity requires more than just an appetite for growth and a good dose of realism. It requires we believe in the opportunity enough to risk our today, and a predictable future, on the unknown.

Unfortunately, the call of opportunity is not always that enticing. How often have organizations met with apathy when rolling out visions of growth? A financial vision of potential returns denuded of the people whose lives will be made better if the company delivers on its promises? Most employees are committed to an organization not because of compensation, but because they believe in what they are doing. Yet they are expected to answer what may feel more like the sirens' call when it is laid out only in numbers: alluring, but empty.

Financial projections are hardly an adequate instrument of motivation. But then Aristotle could have told us as much! His three principles of persuasion—ethos, pathos, and logos—hold the secret to convincing ourselves and others to jump into opportunity with both feet.

Ethos is about the credibility of the source of a message. We are persuaded when we believe in the people from whom a message comes. So who are the real people of opportunity? The ecosystem and consumers. These are the people we need to hear from firsthand, understanding their lives, looking them in the eye and concluding for ourselves that there is need looking for a solution. The people of opportunity are also our colleagues, leaders, and teammates—the people who must buy in if we are to succeed. Their credibility and partnership are critical in deciding to risk our careers, time, or energy on a new venture.

ETHOS

240

> "Don't ask yourself what the world needs. Ask yourself what makes you come alive and then go do that. Because what the world needs is people who have come alive."

Howard Thurman, theologian and human rights activist

PATHOS

Pathos is about passion. It is both personal and communal. It is driven by experience—the joy of invention and discovery, seeing the delight of a consumer, and experiencing the excitement of pursuing our dreams. It is also driven by our values—sparked when we can see the impact of the opportunity—how it will affect the triple bottom line of profits, people, and planet. People are increasingly passionate about big growth that isn't big footprint, that doesn't have downsides for others, that will create lasting value from everlasting resources. When we connect our passions with an opportunity, we will be more deeply committed to seeing it to fruition.

LOGOS

Logos is about a rational belief. It comes from understanding the logic of the opportunity. It goes beyond the columns of a spreadsheet to comprehending how all the pieces of opportunity fit together: how the need, value, and conditions come together, and why the timings are right—envisioning how the opportunity can be shaped and the impact of its shape on its size. It comes from a long view of opportunity; a view of opportunity road maps that show potential competitive response, technological advances, life span of brands, and how we will explore, farm, and mine opportunity in the future. The strategic story of opportunity will both convince and guide us in pursuing opportunity in a sustainable way.

Growth requires the ethos, pathos, and logos of opportunity.

If we want big growth, then we need to see, fully believe in, and act on big opportunity. We need to understand the breadth and depth of opportunity if we are to jump in and create really big ideas that will deliver on that growth.

Grasping the ethos, pathos, and logos of opportunity not only gives us the courage to dive in, it is critical for building the big ideas that will capture opportunity. Developing really Big Ideas—Killer Ideas—requires an equal amount of passion and patience, heart and mind. These precious ideas require the courage to be creative on our own, to fight for ideas, to open ourselves to the inventiveness and creativity of others, and to graft together differentiated offers. They will demand swimming upstream within our organizations and our markets. They require endurance and ingenuity as we care for and cultivate them. Bringing big ideas to fruition requires the patience of a farmer—one who knows that the rewards will be there given the hard work required. Capturing the value from opportunity requires the diligence of the miner—one who doesn't give up after getting the first shiny stuff, but continues to dig deeper because of the reward ahead; and the curiosity of the explorer, always looking out for what might bring new value.

Our growth potential therefore is a direct function of our perception of and commitment to opportunity. And our ability to grasp opportunity is a function of our ability to become Opportunity Thinkers—to see and understand fully the opportunity around us.

OPPORTUNITY THINKING WILL EXPAND HOW WE SEE THE WORLD, OUR ORGANIZATIONS, AND OURSELVES.

When we look at the **WORLD** through the eyes of opportunity, we will see change as an opportunity creator, think in new dimensions, be sensitive to new insights, and build connections with those we meet.

When we look at our **ORGANIZATIONS** through the eyes of opportunity, we will see our common purpose around the core individual we serve, view tensions as the potential for something bigger, and interact with our colleagues as the collaborators they can be.

When we look at **OURSELVES** through the eyes of opportunity, we will see that we have a role to play in opportunity—to explore, farm, or mine it. We will know that only we can play that role, no matter what our position or profession, because we are a unique part of the opportunity ecosystem.

THIS IS WHEN OPPORTUNITY STARTS— WHEN WE OURSELVES BECOME OPPORTUNITY THINKERS.

In the end,
Opportunity Thinking is
the opportunity itself!

It opens our eyes to new possibilities
and launches us on a journey of growth.

LITTLE
EPILOGUE

We live in a different world. It is more open, collaborative, sharing; less about what one person can accomplish and more about what we collectively can achieve. We are each part of many opportunity ecosystems, overlapping, interacting, blending, and separating. For all of these opportunities that we participate in, one thing is true . . . opportunity is not something one person can take credit for. It is the result of countless efforts of discovery and creation.

The opportunities described in this book each have their own ecosystems—the companies named and consumers unnamed, influencers, observers, and, in many cases, we at NewEdge have been involved. We have touched the growth journeys of the majority of companies whose stories you have read. That said, we haven't called out our role because the truth is that everything good which has happened has been a combined effort of ours, the ecosystem, and our clients. All growth is a team sport, all opportunity part of an ecosystem, and all big ideas the result of many contributions. We are happy to be part of so many firms' ecosystems and excited to see the results of our work in their boardrooms and in the hands of consumers—that is the reward.

> " He who receives an idea from me, receives instruction himself without lessening mine; as he who lights his taper at mine, receives light without darkening mine. "
>
> *Thomas Jefferson, former U.S. president and father of the U.S. patent system*

While I have been the storyteller, I am certainly not the only originator of the thinking or stories herein. Our own story is a story of an opportunity ecosystem at its best. It began to crystallize when Paul Stead and I met. Paul is one of the UK's leading designers and business leaders in the design industry. He first grew his company, PSD, to a global force and, after selling it to Cordiant, was appointed CEO of Fitch Worldwide, which at the time was the world's largest design firm. I was a professor at Washington State University doing Disruptive Market Research, a method I had developed using the ecosystem to identify unarticulated needs. I created the method to help Pacific Northwest National Laboratory spin out technology start-ups. At the same time, I was actively publishing internationally on my research on sensory responses to design, taste, scent, etc., which I studied while getting my PhD at the University of Texas at Austin and then led while a professor at Carnegie Mellon University.

A client, Bob Balke, at Eastman Chemical, introduced Paul and me, insisting it would be a big collaboration. Bob was right. I had been looking for a design and go-to-market strategy partner, and Paul had been looking for an insight and business strategy partner. He had just started a new design and strategy firm, The Brewery, and I had just started a new insight and strategy firm, NewEdge.

We quickly joined forces, and the projects came in one after another. There was clearly a hunger for a combined design, insight, and strategy offer; one with deep talents in both business and design and one that clients didn't have to knit together themselves. We brought together, from our pasts, all Six Sources of Growth, Opportunity, and Big Ideas, and formed a partnership that delivers these to clients. I am blessed to have met Paul, who is the ultimate Opportunity Thinker.

Together, we have grown NewEdge and The Brewery, building offices in Richland, Washington near the national lab; Chicago; and London. We have assembled an ecosystem of literally thousands of subject matter experts, trend watchers and trendsetters, leaders, researchers including members of the Industrial Research Institute, and a host of early adopter consumers who give us fresh eyes to see with.

Our clients are really the heroes in this story because they have challenged us with wonderful problems to solve and have opened their organizations to collaborate in discovery and creation. We have traveled the world together, introduced them to our ecosystem, worked long hours on projects, played hard at our Innovation Breweries, instilled Opportunity Thinking through training, and tasted the sweet results of the creative, strategic brewing process.

Paul and I have been fortunate to assemble a team of people able to think in the multiple dialects needed for opportunity. We have business consultants who think creatively and visually and designers who think strategically. They work with 100s of firms, building growth visions, identifying the big opportunities, creating killer ideas, and developing go-to-market strategies, brand communications, and product designs that are both award winning and lead to growth. They have developed Opportunity Thinking training methods for each step, putting new tools in our clients' hands. Every member of our team has influenced the stories and concepts in this book, and for that we are ever grateful.

The story of writing this story is also about an ecosystem.

My family has been my biggest encouragement for both starting and finishing the book. Michael, Bond, Britt, Bryce, and my mother took on my responsibilities, endured my absence, encouraged and cajoled, and then celebrated.

Paul and I continued to develop new ways of visualizing our methods as the story unfolded. A new generation of training tools has emerged as a result.

All the staff members have contributed at one time or another. They have been tough critics and great collaborators. Of particular note though are Aaron Welling, Sonny Virakpanyou, Sarah Hysjulien, Suzanne Vandehey, Nick Lippold, Elizabeth Simmelink, Bailie Kollmar, Mark Putnam, Kristyn Hefelfinger, Erik Whalen-Pedersen, Brittany Davis, Sarah McDonnell, and Matt Thom. Thanks, too, to former colleagues Jamie Stone, Karina Krulig, and Justin Bell.

In addition, the book was strongly influenced by Mark Dickens, a leading UK consultant in retailing and communications. He left an indelible mark on the book's style and tone. He and his wife, Leo, were an inspiration throughout. Brittany Davis was a steadfast encouragement from beginning to end, eclectically inspiring with her diverse reading and thinking, and introducing me to Bartholomew Columbus. Richard Merritt, of Spark Design in Kyrgyzstan, designed the layout and illustrations and was a ton of fun to imagine with. Ed Moore, a historian, consultant, and award-winning sports columnist and editor, both reviewed the examples for accuracy and was the book's editor. Keith Wood helped with insights on mining. Beth Moore and Maryann McChesney-Shaw kept things tidy in the business while my attention was elsewhere. Color Press, Inc. and Nick Lippold of NewEdge did a great job of managing and bringing the project to life. Lew, Ramona, and the rest of my family continually inspire me with their eclectic interests and pursuits.

Finally, I was kept adequately caffeinated during long hours by the team at Espresso World.

My deepest thanks to all of these people and the many others who have encouraged and inspired this story and opened opportunity to me through the years.

INDEX

OPPORTUNITY THOUGHTS

OPPORTUNITY THOUGHTS

259

OPPORTUNITY THOUGHTS

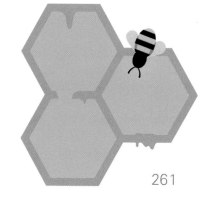

INSIGHTS FROM **OPPORTUNITY THINKING** ADVOCATES

Inspire your journey

> Pam Henderson uses her engaging style to explain that, while ideas may be useful, it is the understanding of opportunities that serves as the real catalyst for growth. It is an approach that is applicable to both companies and individuals, and this delightfully designed book will certainly prove an invaluable guide and inspiration to anyone wanting to get to the next level.

Simon Majumdar
*Author and judge on Food Network's
The Next Iron Chef*

Build bigger ideas

> A thought-provoking read, this book turns individual ideas on their head for true opportunities.

Bob Fisher, Ph.D.
Vice President & CTO, Molson Coors

> NewEdge worked with us to take a concept we thought might have legs and develop it into a big opportunity and then a big idea that has taken off with consumers. In this book you will learn how to do the same.

Aaron Carpenter
Vice President, The North Face

Impact your approach to creativity and innovation

> Don't let its easy-to-read and entertaining approach fool you. It is a deeply thought-provoking book... Pam's insights could have a lasting effect on an organization's way of addressing creativity and innovation.

Klaus Hoehn, Ph.D.
Vice President, John Deere

> Fresh perspective on how you can use observations and trends to chart your future and quickly drive successful innovation.

Steve Revnew
Vice President, The Sherwin-Williams Company

Create a sustainable future

> A fast-paced journey through history, to the modern day and on to the future. We are living in a resource-constrained world. We urgently need new ideas and holistic thinking to seek sustainable opportunities. This book will stimulate this thinking.

John Gardner
Chief Sustainability Officer, Novelis

> Real insight into the challenges of identifying opportunities for Top Line Growth.

Stephen Toton
Vice President, Dupont

Expand how you think

> A novel way of expanding how we think about growth through new ways of seeking opportunity. Pam Henderson weaves modern and historic examples into a journey that inspires you to rethink your current business plan and start anew with a fresh energy and more holistic approach.

Jonathan McIntyre, Ph.D.
Senior Vice President, PepsiCo

...for teams & organizations

"Pam Henderson nails it. A must read for any organization that wants to fully leverage innovation to drive sustainable growth."

Angelo LaGrega
*President, VF Jeanswear
Coalition-Americas
Wrangler, Lee, 7 for all mankind*

"I am going to buy this book for our new product development review group."

John Spero
Six Sigma & Lean Specialist, Praxair

...for non-profits

"Not-for-profit organizations, even faith-based organizations worldwide, can discover in this stimulating and beautifully designed book a turning point which — in a tight economy — can bring them from the urgency of fund-raising and other immediate needs to the priority and integrity of innovation out of opportunity."

Henry A. Paasonen
*Former pastor; Berlin, Paris, Strasbourg
Communications Director international church organization*

...for public agencies

"Breakthrough understanding of Opportunity Thinking that should be required reading for anyone exploring the seemingly mystical realm of innovation. Numerous small vignettes do a wonderful job illustrating the linkages between revolutionary ideas and the opportunities that nourished them. Understanding these relationships is vital for any organization, business, or individual seeking BIG growth!"

Jordan J. Binion
Project Manager, US Army Innovation Lab

...for students

"This book about critical thinking, logic, perspective, and taking action should be required reading for students in a business, marketing, or sales classes, and everyone involved in a business. It provides an opportunity to reflect, challenge current thinking, and engage others in a more creative thinking process. It's provocative, but it's also common sense. It will be referenced by many, and enjoyed by all who break the binding."

Phil Minerich, Ph.D.
Vice President, Hormel Foods

"A veritable cornucopia of facts, experiences, and actionable ideas and insights; studded with numerous pearls and gems of wisdom."

Robert A. Peterson, Ph.D.
*Associate Vice President,
The University of Texas at Austin*

A new kind of book

"Business books are usually a real snooze - not this one. ....The graphics and style are exciting and help the words explode off the pages. Pam has packed super thinking on each page. Don't miss out on this visually entertaining and thought-provoking book. Finally a book on "innovation" that looks and feels innovative."

Frank Harris
President of PDMA, Georgia

"This book is one of the best "opportunities" to unleash the innovation in your organization."

Pat Pinkston
Vice President, John Deere

"Decidedly unlike any business book I can remember... It's like a business book crossed with a Dan Brown novel where you learn many interesting facts along the way!"

Douglas Powell
*Innovation & Product
Development Speaker, LeapInsights*